In *Write to Me*, Basudhara Roy considers a broad sweep of contemporary Indian Poetry in English, coupling the critically incisive eye of an academic with the emotive directness of a poet. The volume's thirty-five essays provide wonderful introductions to the work of the poets reviewed, but along with this they do something more. Collectively, they demonstrate many of the strengths that lie at the heart of the current upsurge of Indian Poetry in English, and beyond this the nature of poetry, in its recent Indian incarnations, itself. The book has its origins in responses to particular volumes of verse, but taken together the reviews serve as a fine introduction to the rich diversity of today's Indian Poetry in English. The voices discussed represent a significant progression from those of the independence generation of Indian poets and it is very rewarding to see them analysed together in this way by a first-rate critic.

- **Prof. John Thieme**
University of East Anglia, UK

To poems from Indians across the country and globe Basudhara Roy brings a wide breadth of reading. It provides a base for close attention to each work that respects the 'mind time' of poems. The critic generously and astutely elucidates their character and concerns in often lyrical prose. If I were publishing a book of poetry, I would want Roy as my reviewer.

- **Prof. Paul Sharrad**
University of Wollongong, Australia

The wide range of books with a diverse flow of ideas, read and discussed by Basudhara Roy reflect her keen insights, her passion for literature and life. The poet in her brings out the essential dynamics of other voices who are equally immersed in the art of writing. The critic in her, with an eye for detail, draws our attention to the metaphors/meanings that make or mar the text. A heart that feels is the one who sees and the one who sees will always seek. *Write to Me* speaking with a curious passion about the power of verse, will mark a new beginning to the world of Indian poetry in English.

- **Prof. Ranu Uniyal**
University of Lucknow, India

Write to Me:
Essays on Indian Poetry in English

Basudhara Roy

BLACK EAGLE BOOKS
Dublin, USA | Bhubaneswar, India

Black Eagle Books
USA address:
7464 Wisdom Lane
Dublin, OH 43016

India address:
E/312, Trident Galaxy, Kalinga Nagar,
Bhubaneswar-751003, Odisha, India

E-mail: info@blackeaglebooks.org
Website: www.blackeaglebooks.org

First International Edition Published by
Black Eagle Books, 2024

WRITE TO ME: ESSAYS ON INDIAN POETRY IN ENGLISH
by **Basudhara Roy**

Copyright © Basudhara Roy

All rights reserved. No part of this publication may be reproduced, stored in a retrieval system, or transmitted, in any form or by any means, electronic, mechanical, photocopying, recording or otherwise without the prior permission of the publisher.

Cover & Interior Design: Ezy's Publication

ISBN- 978-1-64560-543-0 (Paperback)
Library of Congress Control Number: 2024936599

Printed in the United States of America

The world is full of paper.
Write to me.

- Agha Shahid Ali

Acknowledgements

I am deeply grateful to the editors of the numerous journals, magazines, and newspapers in which these essays were first published. Gratitude is owed, in alphabetical order, to *Borderless Journal, Caesurae Mana, Confluence: South-Asian Perspectives, Contemporary Voice of Dalit, Das Literarisch, Different Truths, East India Story, Indialogs; Spanish Journal of India Studies, Indian Literature, Lucy Writers Platform, Muse India, Saaranga Magazine, Scroll, Setu, Teesta Review, The Book Review, The Statesman, The Wire,* and *Times of India*.

My indebtedness rests with Prof. John Thieme of the University of East Anglia, UK, Prof. Paul Sharrad of the University of Wollongong, Australia, and Prof. Ranu Uniyal of the University of Lucknow, India, for going through these essays and for offering encouragement and generous endorsements to light up my efforts.

To friend and mentor Prof. Jaydeep Sarangi, to Mr. Satya Pattanaik of Black Eagle Books, and to all poets and critics who have fed and nourished my love for poetry, my gratitude remains steadfast.

Contents

Introduction	13
Formulating an Ethics of Vulnerability: Bhanu Kapil's *How to Wash a Heart*	21
The Art of Attention: Nishi Pulugurtha's *The Real and the Unreal and Other Poems*	30
Journeying between Worlds: Nitoo Das's *Crowbite*	37
Agony of Speech: Shyamal Kumar Pramanik's *The Untouchable & Other Poems*	43
Across Time, Poetry and Memory: Soni Somarajan's *First Contact*	49
In A Burning Tongue: Soz's *Masculinity Digs a Grave over My Body*	55
Cartograph of Identity: Anita Nahal's *What's Wrong With Us Kali Women?*	62
On the Grave Business of Poetry: GJV Prasad's *This World of Mine: Selected Poems*	71
Meditative Dialogues: Gopal Lahiri's *Alleys are Filled with Future Alphabets: Selected Poems*	76
Unwombing the Mind: Kala Ramesh's *the forest i know*	80

Championing an Identity sans Signifiers: Kalki Subramaniam's *We are Not the Others: Reflections of a Transgender Artivist*	85
Manifestations of Light: Kavita Ezekiel Mendonca's *Light of The Sabbath: Poems about Memories and the sacredness of Light*	94
An Extraordinary Ethics of the Ordinary: Kunwar Narain's *Witnesses of Remembrance*	100
On Writing like a Woman: Paul Kaur's *The Wild Weed*	108
Poised between Contraries: Ram Krishna Singh's *Silence: White Distrust*	112
An Assertion of Sisterhood: Sanjukta Dasgupta's *Unbound: New and Selected Poems*	119
Rebirth of Perception: Shekhar Banerjee's *The Fern-Gatherers' Association*	123
A Romance with Life: Smita Agarwal's *Speak, Woman!*	127
Wo(e)manhood and the Architecture of Feminist Solidarity: Usha Akella's *I Will Not Bear You Sons*	132
Writing Locality as Text: Abhay K's *Monsoon: A Poem of Love and Longing*	140
Sufist Reconstruction of a Broken World: Afsar Mohammad's *Evening with a Sufi: Selected Poems*	144
A Dialogue with Stillness: Bina's *ukiyo-e days… haiku moments*	151

A Marginal Place in Poetry: Jaydeep Sarangi's *letters in lower case*	157
Spatialities of Reflection: Kashiana Singh's *Woman by the Door*	162
The Gospel of the Body: Nilim Kumar's *I'm Your Poet*	167
Where Poetry Meets Enigma: Oindri Sengupta's *After the Fall of a Cloud*	172
The Place of Memory/The Memory of Place: Pramila Venkateswaran's *We are Not a Museum*	177
Tracing a Tiger: Sukrita Paul Kumar's *Vanishing Words*	184
Grief as Vestibule: Vinita Agrawal's *The Natural Language of Grief*	190
A Case for the Body: Kuhu Joshi's *My Body Didn't Come Before Me*	195
The Multiplicity of Heritage: Malashri Lal's *Mandalas of Time*	200
Songs of Redemption: Mitali Chakravarty's *Flight of the Angsana Oriole*	205
The Seductions of Language: Prerna Gill's *Meanwhile*	210
Poetry as Pilgrimage: Robin Ngangom's *My Invented Land*	216
The Palliative of Poetry: Sanket Mhatre's *A City Full of Sirens*	223

Introduction

"Why poetry?", I am often asked, for hasn't Auden famously said, "poetry makes nothing happen"? ('In Memory of W.B. Yeats') Aesthetically speaking, poetry is under no obligation to make anything happen, either in the self or in the world. And yet, one would be hard put to come across poetry that does absolutely nothing. Poetry's essential transgression, as Auden rightly notes, lies in its survival, its ability to effectively guardian and preserve a voice across the transience of life and the ruin and debris of history. By its sheer survival, poetry constitutes a record, a document, a witness, "a way of happening", a timeless "mouth".

Though many regard poetry as making a virtue of inwardness and self-obsession, it is in poetry more than anywhere else in the world that one finds an acute consciousness of the inextricable entanglement between life's private and public domains. Within the staggering diversity of literary and cultural forms, the particular power of poetry comes from its apparent innocuity. Minor, fluid and unassuming, poetry can gently but steadily make its way into, through and across structures of power and authority, seep into their fault lines, and relentlessly make room for questions.

On account of its marginality as a genre, the

transgressive potential of poetry is less obvious, and goes mostly unacknowledged in society. History, however, remains witness to the fact that the clarion call for its most important revolutions have been first articulated in poetry. The reasons for this are not far to seek. Out of the circuit of formal epistemology, poetry has mostly been free to encode and perform alternative knowledges. The language of poetry being generically unanswerable to established patterns of syntax and semantics has, historically, been at liberty to pursue and curate its own ensemble of meaning.

Again, just as poetry, dispensing with literacy and formal training, has offered little resistance or discouragement to potential creators, it has also always been widely accessible to the reading public owing to its capacity for oral dissemination, and for circulation in minor media such as notes, letters, greeting cards, placards and advertisements. But poetry's chief merit, most significantly, lies in its ability to accomplish a multifaceted and compound expression of experience -- one that encompasses reality and possibility, statistics and emotions, and facticity and vision,

Poetry in India and Indian Poetry in English is, currently, going through one of its healthiest and happiest phases. From being an unsure, questionable, and apologetic genre under colonial rule to evolving a distinct idiom, identity, and niche for itself within global readership, IPE today has effectively vernacularized the English language and subtly anglicized the country's *bhashas* through osmotic cultural diversity, linguistic plurality, and the polyphony of imagination.

The visibility of IPE in the larger domain of Indian literature and letters is well-established in the present, thanks to virtual poetry communities, mushrooming online magazines, greater interest in undertaking and reading translations, the support from independent publishing houses, and a greater presence of poets and poetry in literature festivals and award shortlists. The Yearbook of Indian Poetry in English, a series founded by Sukrita Paul Kumar and Vinita Agrawal in the year 2020-21 has been a significant landmark in IPE. With an annual intention to bring together the best pieces of poetry published in English by Indians from the country and its rich diaspora, this anthology has distinctly charged the landscape of IPE by setting up new benchmarks in the evaluation of poetry, and opening up a dialogue between creativity and criticism.

However, the state of criticism within IPE still remains lamentable. It would be difficult to postulate this with statistical exactness but the fact remains that for every hundred or so literary essays produced in the country, poetry barely inspires ten. The majority of poetry books that are published do not get reviewed, and few reviews attempt more than a superficial engagement with poems, altogether eschewing considerations of literary tradition, linguistic lineage, generic innovation, or poetic activism.

Indian Poetry in English needs an able and discursive body of critical discourse to sustain serious attention as a genre. It needs to be taught more committedly in literature classrooms for its full potential to be examined and reaped. Location continues to be a vital concern in academic scholarship today and an effective approach to IPE would be to recognise and read poets from a variety of geo-cultural and linguistic backgrounds. More and diverse poets from the country and its diaspora need to be brought within comparative perspectives, explored in similar and dissimilar contexts, launched into criticism, as also revisited from time to time in order to keep a tradition alive and generously fertile.

Criticism is an inevitable corollary to the act of both producing and consuming literature. All creative pleasure is based on some critical discernment of taste. The very choice of involvement in art, whether as writer or reader, involves a response, however nascent, to essentially critical questions of why, when and how -- the choice and function of genre, its significance to life and the world, and the understanding of literary nuances that evaluates a particular performance as worth or beneath consideration.

In terms of production, once creative frenzy has exhausted itself, it almost involuntarily looks for the guidance and assurance of criticism – do the words on the page read well? Do they qualify as a poem? Do they express to an average reader all that was intended? For the most commonplace of readers too, the enjoyment of a poem is never untouched by the critical impulse since a holistic understanding of a poem is not to be found in itself alone but in placing its receipts within the larger framework of what each reader understands as poetry.

The sustenance of IPE as a fertile literary field demands trained and responsible criticism. As a poet by leaning and academic by training, I have always considered criticism as both art and activism. To critically engage with poetry is to offer to it health and rejuvenation. It is to strengthen both creativity and criticism by placing them in a historical context while also making it possible to see new things within them. It is to boost joy in the act of reading poetry by learning and teaching to identify its subtle beauties, pace, structure, form, ambiguity and freedom.

The essays in this book attempt to address, in their own small way, the significant gap between publication and review, creativity and criticism, and artistic passion and academic activism. These thirty-five pieces were, in their first versions, published independently in a variety of newspapers, magazines, and journals as review responses to the particular books in question, and hopefully offer an useful synchronic statement on IPE. All thirty-five books (except one) were published between 2020 and 2023, a period which, because of the Covid-19 Pandemic, was globally significant in acknowledging the restorative value of poetry as a genre.

The thirty-five poets represented herein perform belonging to a wide range of geographical, cultural and epistemological locations, and have been published by diverse publishing houses, big and small. Geographically, there are poets from the east, west, north, south, north-east of India, and a few from its rich diaspora in the US and Canada. They are women, men, transgenders, immigrants, feminists, sufists, dalit, and they speak from difficult embodiments of deformity, disability, and trauma. Several write originally in English while others have come into the language through the efforts of dedicated translators. For quite a few, these are debut collections while for some others, these are selections from their fertile writing of decades. Here are free verse poems, rhymed pieces, prose poems, ekphrastic poems, and Eastern forms like haiku and tanka. In thematic terms, the range is equally exhaustive with place, history, mythology, ecology, identity, humanism, disease, fear, death, love, survival and more, etched across these pages.

The essays in this book (arranged chronologically according to their four years of publication and within each year, alphabetically arranged by names of authors) intend to be a gentle companion to reading and appreciating poetry. There are innumerable points of entry into a book of poems just as there are innumerable points to meet a river's water. These essays show pathways that I have taken in my journey as a reader, not so that other readers will stick to them but so that they might be enticed and encouraged to find their own independent pathways of engagement with poetry. In their wish to be interesting rather than intimidating, these essays contain little jargon and almost no critical terminology that an uninitiated reader of poetry might not be familiar with.

As their tone and form will amply illustrate, these are not academic essays. Their purpose is to help readers to make sense of poetry in general, and to enjoy and appreciate these thirty-five books of poetry in particular. Intended for attentive, leisurely reading, *Write to Me* (its title gratefully borrowed from Agha Shahid Ali's well-known poem 'Stationery') aspires to invite the uninitiated reader into poetry and to spur the initiated reader into the finer aspects of reading and listening to poems. Above all, the book wishes to be pleasurable -- to woo readers to poetry, to the criticism of poetry, and to the possibility of poetry in criticism.

No art can ever be solitary, for art itself is a communicative act -- an eternal address to human loneliness. It is a reminder of community, kinship, and the possibility of transcending isolation. As a poet, it is important to engage with one's times by observing, documenting, critically appreciating and promoting the works of one's contemporaries. Every essay here is a reader's return-gift for the love, joy and beauty that I have received from poetry. My greatest hope in bringing these essays together as a book is that this love, joy and beauty is passed on to the world.

Formulating an Ethics of Vulnerability: Bhanu Kapil's *How to Wash a Heart*

For every reader acquainted with the work of Bhanu Kapil, an arrival to her writing is integrally accompanied with the readiness to be surprised. *How to Wash a Heart* (Liverpool University Press, 2020) is no exception. The title, in all its neatness, unsettles. Why, one broods, would it be necessary to wash a heart? Would that be a clinical image? Or, might it not, with all its purgative echoes, qualify for a spiritual one? The indifferent precision of the title's tone reminding the reader of the numerous self-help/DIY manuals in the world complicates matters further, engendering a distinct contemplative chaos.

When you meet the forty untitled poems in the book, they astound as much by what they say as by what they don't. And this is not accomplished through compression, obliqueness or understatement alone but by a highly configured use of language operating at a densely symbolic level. Silence is, aurally, visibly and psychically, an important textual component in this collection. With each poem being roughly around twenty lines and uninterrupted by titles, the written text on the page seems to establish a direct and deliberate spatial relationship with blankness – a relationship that brims with the possibility of both the fertile and the fatal.

In reading the poems and in taking cue from the highly imagistic 'Note on the Title' by Kapil, a definitive narrative emerges. Here is "an attempt to work out a relationship" between "an immigrant guest in the home of their citizen host". The speaker in this collection, it is emphasized, is an artist – a fact that increases the speaker's vulnerability. The narrative derives some impetus from the writer's having come across an article about a white Californian couple with an adopted daughter from the Philippines and their offering of "a room in their home to a person with a precarious visa status". The white woman's "ornate way of describing the hospitality that she was offering" and something about the tautness of her facial muscles as she smiled in the photograph seemed, to the author, to be contradicting each other. This conflict between host and hostility on the one hand, and hospitable and hospital on the other, becomes the terse narrative motif of *How to Wash a Heart* -- a perspective that has largely been nourished by Kapil's own experiences as a non-white academic in the United States, encountering "an outward-facing generosity or inclusivity that had not, always, matched the lived experience".

""It's not the men who exile me,/ It's the women. I don't trust/ The women," wrote/ Aurora Levins Morales" states one of the poems. Explored in this collection is a tangible web of relationships between women and the world -- the immigrant woman artist's relationship to her host, her relationship to the host's adopted daughter, her relationship to her own immigrant past, her relationship to art, and her relationship, ultimately, to the globalized social world where many complex forms of violence thrive unabated. As the first poem states, the "keywords" here are "Hospitality, stars, jasmine, Privacy." The arrangement is telling. While 'hospitality' is what the host presumes to offer and 'privacy' is what the guest expects to receive, bracketed between them are the Occidental 'star' and the Oriental 'jasmine', making the entire line appear like a neat binary with two categories each or a semantic arrangement in descending order of value.

Identity is an overarching theme within the collection and as the poems establish, it is an entity continually under duress. One's identity, at any point of time, is determined by too many factors beyond one's control and is constantly in the un/making. For the immigrant artist, trauma lies in her host's imposition of an overworn racial stereotype on her lived/living self, and her inability to see her in her vulnerable individuality. Her confessions are straightforward: "I come from a country/ All lime-pink on the soggy map." "My spiritual power was quickly depleted/ By living with you." The presence of racial difference in the new home in the shape of the host's Filipino daughter (described by her mother as "an Asian refugee") makes the immigrant speaker feel "less like a hoax". "I don't want to beautify our collective trauma," she says and yet this is what she must keep learning to do as a welcome guest.

The forty poems that shape themselves via the consciousness of this non-white artist become an intimate documentary of psychological trauma and the subtle kinds of erasures that immigrants are routinely subjected to in white spaces:

The messages we received
Were as follows:
You are a sexual object, I have a right
To sexualize you.
You are not an individual.
You are here For my entertainment.
Or in another poem where she says:
I can smell your body
Odor.
I can smell your vagina.
Are you wearing your genitals
As a brooch?

The attempt to overwrite identity, one notes, is carried out throughout the collection, on the material site of the body -- "Shame invites the sun/ To live in the anus, the creases/ Of the throat"; the white city becomes "A grey ribbon tied around the wrist" of the immigrant, gradually growing taut; and sometimes, with "a voice/ That was too loud", the host rudely interrupts the immigrant artist's reveries. The body, for Kapil, constitutes a vital receptor of the responses of the world. Its needs, no matter where it is placed, are constant, predictable, intimate and insistent, and it is in their being met or denied that one feels, by turns, homed and homeless. It is partly, therefore, to increase the body's tenacity that its regulating organ, the heart, needs to be symbolically removed, washed and replaced at regular intervals.

What makes the immigrant experience more layered in this collection is the interaction of three personal racial histories of the three women here, and the psycho-cultural subtexts of home, family and parenting that effortlessly emerge as relationship metaphors in this sociological encounter, only to be violently subverted and vandalized of, even, their native meanings. Images of m/othering loom large over these poems and the power equation between the host and the guest is partly illustrated through that hierarchy. The host offers care as an "intrusive mother", buys her "pretty bras" but also 'bangs' the cup down by her sleeping person, wields silence like 'an axe raised over the head' and can hardly be trusted ("...I never knew/ When you might open my door, leaving it open/ When you left.") because

> this is your house
> And there's no law
> That requires
> What you're offering me to last
> Or outlast
> The moment I crossed your threshold

The collection assumes a surreal quality as the intrusive mother-figure in the host coalesces with the 'conditional caregiving' biological mother who, in the speaker's memories, stuck wet caps of okra to her young daughter's "forehead, cheeks and nose", and to compound all these is the lurking suspicion of whether a mother, at all, exists – "Or like a baby crawling on the bumpy/ Carpet, am I my own/ Mother, actually?"

As one moves through the book, home, as a signifier, loses its stability and concreteness, becomes free floating, infirm, and an infirmary of sorts:

> The art of crisis
> *Is that you no longer*
> Think of home
> As a place for social respite.
> Instead, it's a ledge
> Above a narrow canyon.

The danger is unignorable in these lines as the

comfort zone emotively signified by home transforms into a mere niche of survival, any other version of it causing only shame and fear in this new world -- "It's extraordinary how afraid I am/ All the time."

Inhabiting the psyche of Kapil's poems are significant existential questions. What is a home? Has such a space ever existed? Is it wise, then, to mourn its lack? How does art feed on life and vice-versa? *"How do you live when the link/ Between creativity/ And survival/ Can't easily/ Be discerned?" "Are these questions enough/ To violate/ Your desire for art/ That comes from a foreign/ Place?"* Does the Filipino daughter experience her home in the same way as the immigrant artist does? *"What are the limits/ Of this welcome?"* Does the bonding between her immigrant guest and her Asian refugee daughter make the host feel insecure? *"Without words,/ Your daughter and I/ Drank water/ From the bowls on the windowsill,/A traditional form/ Of consumption."* Is the host's ultimate betrayal of her guest an attempt to reclaim her daughter? *"Your daughter is screaming./ My eyes are on fire"*

Belying the enunciative methodical promise of the title, the narrative that these poems enclose is highly chaotic, disjunctive and determinedly evasive. Here is an interaction of complex histories and the inability of individuals to countenance them with clarity, understanding or empathy. Language is a vital site for Kapil's intellectual and creative experimentation, and a continuous interrogative terrain for positing and unpacking statements of identity. Sparse, terse, and highly imagistic, her language functions, often, as still, clear water faithfully performing its role of reflecting the mind's brisk tectonic movements. Animated with the aesthetics and politics of her performative work, Kapil's language takes on an agility that allows for its sustained sharpness without compromising its lyrical grace, rendering it, thereby, both incessantly combative and redemptively poetic. Consider these lines:

> I could not bear the facial expressions
> Of the people
> I was closest to, a source
> Of embarrassment.
> And so I left,
> Never to return
> Intact.
> Or to a home
> That was intact.

Or these lines from another poem:

> My secret is this:
> Though we lost all our possessions,
> I felt
> A strange relief
> To see my home explode in the rearview mirror.

The line breaks are highly unusual here. On close listening, however, one realizes that this clipped manner retains the performative rage, audacity and spontaneity of the spoken language. There is a gnawing poignancy in Kapil's style accompanied, in her best poems, by a sedative seduction that emotionally overwhelms even as it spiritually illuminates. Her register is wide, her metaphors well-processed, and her wits sharp. Note how, in the following lines, the dwarfing and gradual erasure of the immigrant's identity is presented through the metaphor of an envelope:

> The host-guest chemistry Is inclusive, complex, molecular,
> Dainty.
> Google it.

> Does the host envelop
> The guest or does the guest
> Attract diminished forms
> Of love....

There is a palpable sense of dis-ease in *How to Wash a Heart*, an overwhelming existential claustrophobia that addresses the world's unforgiving contradictions beyond the 'native host-immigrant guest' dialectic, and whether the speaker facing the world in these poems were interrogating ableism, heterosexuality, genderism or anthropomorphism, the angst would remain the same. Here is a trauma as much historical as it is personal and social, constituting an inviolate kernel of the transgressive yet inevitable self/other relationship. Splintering as these poems are, they remain, at the same time, undeniably therapeutic. By calling for special attention to the heart in both medical and emotive terms, Kapil seems to be arguing for our essential and shared vulnerability as a global society, for a keener acceptance of our physical, mental and cultural differences, and for a more humane and humanistic social discourse.

Theorizing the integral public dimension of our personal bodies, Judith Butler, in *Precarious Life*, writes, "The body implies mortality, vulnerability, agency: the skin and the flesh expose us to the gaze of others, but also to touch, and to violence, and bodies put us at risk of becoming the agency and instrument of all these as well. Although we struggle for rights over our own bodies, the very bodies for which we struggle are not quite ever only our own. The body has its invariably public dimension." Kapil's poems culturally perform this public dimension of the body, urging us to ethically identify all bodies everywhere as our shared responsibility.

Derived from the Latin 'vulnus' meaning 'wound', vulnerability constitutes an essential recognition of our subjection to power and violence, and of our inherent inability to avoid, counter or overcome it as humans. Having been inoculated by the profound vulnerability of these poems and by their intense pain and beauty, the heart is purged of apathy once and for all, and an expanded awareness of being-in-the-world dawns -- "Because living with someone who is in pain/ Requires you to move in a different way".

The Art of Attention: Nishi Pulugurtha's *The Real and the Unreal and Other Poems*

"To reach a geographic frontier, one needs only a strong pair of legs; to reach an intellectual frontier, one needs a trained mind," writes geographer Yi-fu Tuan. To arrive at an emotional frontier, one needs, I would add, an ever empathetic imagination and an enhanced level of attention to the world that weaves itself continually around our bodies and minds. The translation of sensory experience into emotive fact calls for an orientation of sight, experience and vision that leads, in turn, to a nuanced accomplishment of the act of attention. When allied with spiritual integrity, respect for life and a higher sense of selfhood, attention becomes an art that helps illumine the world with tenderness and faith.

To find one's way into the poetry of Nishi Pulugurtha is to enter just such a realm of heightened attention. The depth of detail here is so staggering that it amounts to a certain self-reflexiveness of thought. In the sixty bafflingly simple poems in her debut collection, *The Real and the Unreal and Other Poems* (Authorspress, 2020), one confronts a wide landscape of quiet, contented silence where thoughts concentrate on their own finesse and life's greatest complexities are steadily unwound into tender understanding and mature resignation. "I write on almost anything and everything that catches my eye, that sets me thinking, that makes me express," states Pulugurtha. "Just about anything that strikes me and remains with me." Her subjects are many and free-ranging – "from nature, to children playing in the streets, to a plant growing through the masonry, to the flowers blooming in my pots, to solitude and silence, to the masks we wear, to places that I have visited and how they stay on with me, to nostalgia and memory, to the myriad changes that life is all about and life in these trying times." Composed mainly during the first wave of the pandemic in India, the quietness in these poems take on a deeper autumnal shade. Silence, distance, isolation and suffering are not romantic choices here but the coordinates of a difficult world. In 'The Locked Workplace', the poet visualizes her workplace as another home suffering from lockdown loneliness:

> foliage all around
> overgrown maybe
> unkempt too
> empty corridors, empty stairs
> a musty smell from the closed rooms
> thick layers of dust everywhere
> the gate closed, the creepers wild
> the grass untidy
> cobwebs too, in places
> as we remain locked in
> at home

'Walking Home' is a poignant articulation of the plight of migrant workers in India in that phase:

> the city had been his home for some years
> leaving his family he moved here
> for work, for sustenance
> he lived in a room with four others
> cramped, but a place to sleep.
> and then it happened
> he had to leave
> his belongings, just a few basics
> the bag on his back, he sets off
> there were more like him
> they were going home

In 'The City has No Room for Us' the contrast between the workers' understanding of the city as home and their forced return to the place the city looks upon as their home, bespeaks a deep pain of betrayal.

In poem after poem in the collection, the reader is both enticed and amazed by the poet's intense desire to look at things straight in the eye, without metaphor and thoroughly without trappings. In the title poem of the volume, Pulugurtha marvels at how the world has remained the same throughout the flow of ages:

> to see and ignore
> to conceal, to lie
> to bluff, to fight against known
> and unknown enemies
> harbouring all around
> waiting to pierce, to stab
> to hurt
> to wreck, to destroy
> to ruin, to reveal
> the truth, ugly and bizarre
> unreal yet real.

The relationship between fact and fiction has been so swapped that one is no more convinced of a boundary line between the real and the unreal.

Consistently at work in this book is a poetic lens that is largely photographic. "Nishi Pulugurtha," as the eminent poet-critic Sanjukta Dasgupta rightly reminds us in her Foreword to the book, "is a widely published travelogue writer. In fact, the poems stand out due to their descriptive brilliance and due to the sincere reflections on sights and sounds, feelings and emotions, sometimes resigned, sometimes transcendent." Pulugurtha's poems document the world in its stark realism without complaint or regret. One meets here life's immensity, its large-scale variety and its everyday injustices – both great and small. If nature is kind, life is often not. In poems like 'Moyna', 'Anu and Moyna' and 'Mela', the unkindness of life is almost unbearable. Yet, the poet's attitude towards it is unmarked by anger or despair. Brave with fortitude, she calmly and analytically examines life's various facets and penetrates to the depths of its truths only to leave them untouched when found. In 'Bitter Gourd', for instance, she writes:

> Among all the dirt, there it was
> Pushing back so much of the unwanted
> Breaking out
> Pushing
> Carving a small place
> Being seen
> Uncared but there.

"Uncared but there" is a motif that emerges powerfully from *The Real and the Unreal and Other Poems*. To the poet, this tendency of nature to follow her own particular rhythms despite human indifference is both lesson and wisdom. Pulugurtha's poems, the reader will realize, locate themselves in the palimpsest of the everyday. Her subjects are rooted in the routine of her regular life. Traced through her photographic clarity, however, the most mundane details acquire a startling newness. One is infected by the sheer wonder of the perception that contours the world it inhabits with an almost child-like faith. In 'It Does Find a Way', she writes of a small plant's resilience:

> Beside a wall that separates
> The small plant seeps through
> Breaking through a gap
> Creating a crevice
> Wild and green
> It stands up steady
> Breaking through the masonry
> It does find a way somewhere, somehow

The landscape of her poems is decidedly urban, yet hemmed and embroidered powerfully by nature's benevolence. These pockets of trees, plants, flowers, rivers, dilapidated structures and firm ruins constitute the perches of Pulugurtha's consciousness. Amidst the regular bustle, breathlessness and uncertainty of life, it is the predictability and promise of these sites that anchor the poet's sanity. The range of emotions these poems take us through is staggering. There is agony at life's injustices, pain at the loss of familiar landmarks, hurt at the world's selfishness and disregard, and loud assertions of a powerful female selfhood in a patriarchal world. But above all, these poems stand out for their eco-conscious sensibility and their sense of repose in nature's bounty of colour, form and wisdom.

Blending memorably into the spirit of this collection are the ten concluding 'Dementia Poems' that earnestly articulate the restlessness, poignancy and shadows of a mind battling dementia in a world where psycho-physical frailty and disability find little support. Having worked firsthand with Alzheimer and Dementia patients and having published extensively on them, Pulugurtha brings a deep understanding of the subject into her poetry. Underlining these ten poems is a continual sense of search, a staunch desire to hold on to life while resuscitating the past in memory and a strict belief in the reclamation of peace as life's singular treasure. The essential physical particulars of life are, however, nearly always lost leading to a perpetual sense of vacuum. Accompanying such agonies of memory are the omnipotent physical pulls of exhaustion, hunger and sleep that the poems tenderly chart, echoing in their utter simplicity, an irreparable sense of grief.

Pulugurtha's forte, I will choose to advance, is predominantly, the narrative. Though descriptions loom large over her poetic canvas, the tripod on which her descriptive camera is placed is the tripod of narrative whose intention is to tell the tale unerringly as it is. Her poetic style involves neither proposing nor disposing but recording things as they manifest themselves in association with each other. It is characteristic of Pulugurtha's style that having explored the visual dimensions of a subject in poetry, she does not dramatically agonize over metaphoric ramifications but quietly lets the poem rest with an observation that in its profundity, manifests itself often as an understatement. One poem after another will leave the reader with an unsettled sense of peace, with a loss biting at the roots of the heart, with a reconciliation that is tragically incomplete. It is in this documentation of life's essential incompleteness that Pulugurtha undeniably accomplishes her calling as a poet, for did not the great Basho say, "The invincible power of poetry has reduced me to the condition of a tattered beggar"?

Journeying between Worlds: Nitoo Das's *Crowbite*

In her essay, 'Woman and Bird' in *What is Found There: Notebooks on Poetry and Politics*, Adrienne Rich describes her sudden sighting of a magnificent Great Blue Heron, a bird she has never seen from close quarters before and this brief encounter leads her on to a dialogic exploration of "all the times when people have summoned language into the activity of plotting connections between, and marking distinctions among, the elements presented to our senses" 6, of the potentiality of making such experiences the means of interpretation of poetry and life. Concluding the essay, Rich writes,

Neither of us—woman or bird—is a symbol, despite efforts to make us that. […] I made no claim upon the heron as my personal instructor. But our trajectories crossed at a time when I was ready to begin something new, the nature of which I did not clearly see. And poetry, too, begins in this way: the crossing of trajectories of two (or more) elements that might not otherwise have known simultaneity. When this happens, a piece of the universe is revealed as if for the first time.

One of the apparent reasons that this essay comes

to my mind after reading Nitoo Das's third collection of poetry, *Crowbite* (Red River, 2020), is of course the fact that both these writings are undeniably watermarked by the experience of birdwatching. On a deeper and more subtle level, however, what strikes me is the way in which *Crowbite* profoundly echoes Rich's idea of poetry here – "the crossing of trajectories of two (or more) elements that might not otherwise have known simultaneity" and its revelation of a piece of the universe that has been scarcely known in the same way before.

As powerful as they are beautiful, as experimental as they are traditional, and as astounding as they are soothing, the thirty poems in this collection will take the reader on a journey that begins concretely in place and culminates in an existential place-less-ness that haunts both without and within. Close attention to topography is an important feature of Das's poetry and each poem in *Crowbite* is testimony to the poet's intimate communication and engagement with the landscape of her hometown in the hills. While even a cursory glance at the titles in the book reveals an intense grounding of most of these poems in a physical locale - Mawphlang, Laitkynsew, Tawang, NEHU, Ka Kshaid Lai Pateng Khohsiew, Mawlynnong, Mawsmai Caves, Sohra and Thukje Chueling Nunnery, all poems here are undoubtedly contextualized in a well-defined geographical space. Arne Naess in *Life's Philosophy* writes, "There is a telling German word, *Merkwelt*, for which the closest English equivalent is "everything that a definite being is aware of." When it comes to landscape poetry, Das's *Merkwelt* is profoundly rich and she can penetrate the ostensible and concrete in it to arrive at the unusual and remote. In the poem 'Root Bridge, Mawlynnong', for instance, roots find their being in a metaphor from the world of fiction:

These roots are words that many hands have looped into a tale

With dangling subplots, conflicts, an infinite resolution and characters constantly fucking.

In 'Spotting a Spotted Forktail', the "yin-yang bird" acquires an unusually graphic description:

> He sprints
> like the scattered prints of a newspaper.
> he is a chess game speckled
> with dots. A zebra bird
> with strategic fullstops.
> A monochrome
> forktrailing a contrast
> where the Rhododendron drops.

Markers – geographical, cultural and linguistic – galore in *Crowbite* as the North-East assumes its significant presence as a protagonist within this collection and as the poems themselves take on the serenity and wonder of the landscape they describe. However, it won't take the reader long to realize that Das's poetry, though, it stems from a territorial response to being and belonging in physical space, enacts itself essentially in the mind. Her landscape, rich though it is, telescopes almost inevitably into her mindscape and it is from this that her images acquire their rich visceral quality.

Examine, for instance, the opening and closing poems of the collection. The opening poem, 'Mawphlang' begins with a physical forest that threatens constantly to slide inwards:

The forest is something indecisive
between twig and soil.
It is an old woman opening
her mouth. She has nothing to reveal.

The closing piece, 'The Cat's Daughters', as surreptitious, as mysterious and as metaphysical as the cat itself, closes with a journey that is decidedly inwards, a call towards primordiality, a return to the womb:

We imagine
our mother aging. We worry about her. She tells us:
If the basil dies and the milk curdles, come
save me. And so,
the basil dies and the milk curdles
and we go off on our travels. No,
we marry neither the merchant
nor the river prince. We birth
neither pestles
nor pumpkins. We want to find
our mother, see her silver eyes, touch
her old fur,
kiss her fish-mouth again.

It is this essential spatial tension between the landscape and the mindscape that accounts for a very different sense of temporality in Das's poems, a fact that strikes one quite early into *Crowbite*. Though these poems are nourished by a deep affinity towards the natural world, the temporal rhythm they owe their allegiance to is neither chronological nor geological but purely intellectual, something I would call, mind time. Whether, it is observing a forktail, a leaf, a waterfall, an elephant, the rhododendrons, a painting or even a bus, Das's reflections follow their own trajectory, their unique ratiocinative beat and it is through the subconscious meeting of these trajectories that her powerful poetry is born.

Poems like 'Leaf in My Room' and 'In Which Mawlynnong is a Fractal' are brilliant poetic ratiocinations explored through questions and answers. While in the former, each answer leads to more questions and in the latter, the questions don't stop for answers, in both the poems we are brought only and amply close to the understanding of language's failure to ask or answer, and in turn, to know or mirror the world. And this overpowering awareness of the powerlessness of language to make sense of the world is perhaps what bestows its greatest strength to Nitoo Das's poetry.

Devdutt Pattnaik in his article 'The Song of the Crow' writes:

The word 'why' is translated as ka in Sanskrit, the sacred language of Hinduism. Ka is the first consonant of the Sanskrit language. It is both an interrogation as well as an exclamation. It is also one of the earliest names given to God in Hinduism. During funeral ceremonies, Hindus are encouraged to feed crows. The crow caws, "Ka?! Ka?!" It is the voice of the ancestors who hope that the children they have left behind on earth spend adequate time on the most fundamental question of existence, "Why?! Why?!" In mythology there is a crow called Kakabhusandi who sits on the branch of Kalpataru, the wish-fulfilling tree. The tree fulfills every wish but is unable to answer Kakabhusandi's timeless and universal question, "Ka?! Ka?!"

Though the eponymous and incredibly moving poem 'Crowbite' in the book is engendered within a different cultural mythology and worldview, the crow remains here, as elsewhere, a "cawcawcaw of black" a cry connecting the soul to the earth. a question-mark on civilization, a suspicion, a misgiving, a patch of darkness on the possibility of knowledge, an epistemological interrogation, a stark reminder of human vulnerability. In the closing lines of the poem, the crowbite that pursues Bhobai like both prophecy and legacy, becomes a metaphor not just for creative freedom but also existential freedom. It is freedom from civilization and its hierarchies of truth and knowledge, a crossing over of boundaries – from physical to metaphysical, and an affirmation of the ultimate embodiment of the world. Bhobai the man becoming Bhobai the crow acquires a(n) in/sight that is terribly human and yet beyond the scope of the average, fallible human:

I went wherever I wanted to. I looked at people's eyes and knew their secrets. I sang songs with the fishermen. I bathed in the sacred river and flew away from their temples before they could throw stones at me.

The beautiful designing of the book accentuates the tactile and visceral quality that inhabits these poems. Not to be missed are the remarkable illustrations by the poet that by bringing in another dimension of visuality and experience, lend a sinewy force to the overall interpretation of *Crowbite*.

Agony of Speech: Shyamal Kumar Pramanik's *The Untouchable & Other Poems*

In *Can Literature Promote Justice?*, Kimberly A. Nance writes:

> This is the difference between the poetics and the prosaics. Poetics is the realm of the imagination and of multiple possibilities, while prosaics is the realm of concrete choices and of consequences. Deliberative *testimonio* finally does offer something to its audience: neither purity nor certainties but rather lessons in how to construct, maintain, critique, and when necessary change a set of essentially contestable foundations that help to decide what to do at each of those points of decision—a do-it-yourself ethics.

What does a collection of poems that stands witness to not just its speaker-narrator-poet's private life but to an entire historiography of his society, culture and times, have to offer us by way of knowledge? Factual information, certainly, but more than that what poetry lays bare to its readers is the epistemology of the soul, the emotive geography of being and experience, and the imaginative possibility of transcendence and change. In poetry more than prose, is felt the acute striving towards possibilities, the ethics of envisioning, and the cartographic formulation of a subjectivity that endears and inspires by its consistent honesty and truth. Reading *The Untouchable & Other Poems* (Authorspress, 2020) by the Bengali Dalit activist, Shyamal Kumar Pramanik, translated from the original Bengali by writer-academics, Jaydeep Sarangi and Anurima Chanda, leaves the reader with an experience that is as heart-wrenching as it is transformative and memorable.

Belonging to the Poundra Kshatriya community, one of the major Scheduled Caste communities in West Bengal with a bitter history of discrimination and abuse against it, Pramanik articulates, in his poetry, the quintessential Dalit voice characterized by rage, defiance, resilience and hope. For Pramanik, as he states in the interview that prefaces his poems, the term 'dalit' refers to "those people from the depressed classes who are exploited socially and economically on the basis of their birth, by the system of Manuism and Brahmanism as propagated under the Hindu religion." Kneaded out of a cultural experience of pain, slavery, victimization, oppression, humiliation and injustice, Pramanik's poems uphold the Dailt literary thinking that caste is not an obsolete inheritance of the past being borne, cross-like, in the present but a burning social issue in contemporary India. Like race, gender and sexuality, caste remains a subtle form of everyday power exercised through definition, discrimination and surveillance. As a Dalit activist, Pramanik expresses his staunch commitment to envision and bring about a casteless society – "to establish equality and fraternity among Indians, irrespective of their caste and religion." The fifty poems that comprise *The Untouchable & Other Poems* are strong, evocative expressions of revolt and self-assertion against a hegemonic savarna culture that thwarts at each turn the identity and aspirations of the lower castes. These poems, writes Pramanik, "are based on my holistic autobiographical experiences, and are not about a particular kind of Dalit experience." The Dalit autobiographical mode of writing, while it is expressive of personal emotions, articulates a communal representation of the experience of suffering and deprivation and constitutes a valuable socio-political document that both archives and subverts the status of victimization and control.

Examine the very first poem of the volume, 'I Know':

I know
I know everything is right.
Yet I didn't face you upright.
I sit in the turn of the road,
Heart full of sufferings.
I look at the Eastern sky
Watch the rise of
The fourth world from the dark.

The very title, 'I Know', in its assertion of knowledge, historical, social, cultural, and political, subverts the logic of domination in claiming a free subjecthood. In this English translation, the semantic juxtaposition of 'right' and 'upright' with connotations of in/justice and oppression and the hopeful promise of the dark, largely sets the tone of Pramanik's oeuvre. One finds embodied here all the ideas that watermark this intricate and urgent volume of poems - the consciousness of the liminality of space, the essential Dalit double consciousness, a sensitivity to the natural world as a repository of wisdom and harbinger of change, linguistic and ideological resistance and, above all, the looking forward to change - slow but definite.

The spatial exclusion of Dalits as a social group has affected their discrimination and identity in marked ways. Pramanik's poems evince such spatial consciousness in diverse and complex ways. To begin with, there is the immediate physical/geographical space from where the poet speaks – "a mud house" in the soil of his birth in "one of India's backward villages" which is marked by "a restricted sky", a "secluded river bank", "surrounded by shit and vomit". Permeating this geographical space is the cultural space of family memories and folklores, community gatherings, rituals and patterns of celebration:

> We had families and homes here
> My own people lived by this old waterscape
> We used to sing songs of Maa Shitala staring at each other
> Used to watch Kalpurush at night.

Compounding these spatial dimensions is the poet's acute awareness of inhabiting a space that extends beyond the personal to the socio-historical. The personal pronoun 'I' in his poems, easily lapses into a shared 'we' that is sharply demarcated against a 'they' that believed themselves to be "equipped with Brahmatya", a blind, malevolent 'they':

> They who had destroyed our houses
> They who had destroyed our lives
> Played Holi with our blood
> And they, who did not speak
> They saw but did not see

Looming large over these poems is the poet's acute double-consciousness of his lot and his realization of the need to reconcile the category of Dalit with the universal human on the one hand and the particular Indian on the other. In 'My Existence in Ruins', for instance, he writes:

All my life I have searched for our civilization's ancient history
In the spread of this land's depths
In never-ending dreams.
Am I such a nobody!

The reader is startled in these poems by a language that resists, both aesthetically and functionally, the materiality of subjugation and the incarceration of the imagination by bending its standard syntax and semantics in unthought of ways. What must not be missed in this coding of resistance is Pramanik's acute consciousness of the natural world from which most of his images of upheaval, transgression and resurrection are drawn. Though almost every poem in this volume brings in images of the natural splendour of the rural Bengal countryside, nature far more than a mere background to Pramanik's poetry, is of essential ideological and aesthetic value within it. Firstly, the natural world manifests itself to the poet as both companion and refuge in his relentless struggle with inequality. It represents, secondly, the principle of destruction, renewal and change, offering a vision to the poet that this phase of social victimization too shall pass. Thirdly, it is a trope of continuity, linking the poet to his community and the community to its history. This is a site where temporal distinctions diffuse and the past, present and future coalesce to foster experience, wisdom and hope. Finally, and most importantly, a kinship with nature allows the poet to reclaim the space of primitivity and primordiality which is beyond the discriminatory logic of civilization and culture. This, then, is the poet's utopia towards which he strives. The poem, 'Here, Earth Narrates its Birthstory', envisions a return to a pristine geological glory where the essential humanity of man glows untarnished:

And Kalpurush comes walking from another planet-
He tells me of songs sung by enlightened birds,
Tales of primordial rocks and ancient forests;
A wondrous worldly life emerging out of destruction.
Awake, awake O world's primitive man.

In the Preface to this collection, the translators, Jaydeep Sarangi and Anurima Chanda aptly remark that Pramanik's poetry, "does not simply manifest itself in torrid descriptions of Dalit life. Rather, it attempts to derive out of these experiences a new value system that would help Dalits to carve out a new social reality." Pramanik's poems, despite their moving agony and insistent rage, assert the predominance of hope and unwavering faith in a better tomorrow. It is impossible to not mention the authenticity and remarkable fluidity that characterizes these translations, the translators having negotiated deftly and creatively between two different linguistic and ideological systems to ensure that vital meanings are retained, both factually and stylistically. A word also must be said for the gifted illustrator, Arpita Pandey, whose illustrations offer new metaphors for the aesthetic exploration of these urgently beautiful poems.

Across Time, Poetry and Memory: Soni Somarajan's *First Contact*

> It's odd how I demystify the sea,
> to the point of a billion random matings of two elements:
> triptychs of them falling into place,
> as if life's memory knows the sun must slake its thirst.
> The lifespan of a pregnant cloud,
> cut short by a bulwark of hills, sheds weight to earth.
> The sea is a reminder —
> the amniotic origin of creation.
> - Soni Somarajan, 'Our First Home'

Approaching a debut collection of poems normally gears one for certain expectations. A tender nascence foreshadows the word 'debut'. There is in it a certain suggestion of tentativeness, of eagerness, hasty flamboyance. One is prepared to encounter restlessness, quick enthusiasm, as also, a sense of surfeit. Making way through the pages of Soni Somarajan's debut collection *First Contact* (Red River, 2020), however, one's impression of the word 'debut' is altered for ever. A permanent semantic shift takes place on the terrain of experience as one meanders through the sixty-five distilled poems that comprise the book and by the time the concluding poem has had its say, the word 'debut' has translated itself in the mind from 'invitation' to mean 'arrival'. I realize that a debutante's tentative invitation to the world can equally mean an announcement of an accomplished artist's arrival.

In the work of Soni Somarajan, one undeniably meets an artist who has been preparing himself for poetry for a long time now and whose commitment to it is unswerving. Here is a poet who builds his world brick by brick, memory by memory, word by word – every choice as attentive as it is authentic. These are poems that have emerged from the depths of honest reflection on the self and the ways in which it coheres in the world. In his short, compact and illuminating note 'Why I Write Poetry', Somarajan states:

For the past thirty years, I've borne the brunt of a progressive neuromuscular disorder. Two-thirds of this time, I've made do with a permanent sidekick: a wheelchair. It's almost as if I've accessed a parallel world. Quite naturally, I yearned to express this experience. […] Poetry, I realize, is the finest way to express myself and my fading past. I recognised its unique ability to speak for me in ways inconceivable. […] With poetry, I began to record my two lives – a memoir in verse.

The collection, indeed, manifests itself as a rare piece of life writing in verse. Other than the theme poem 'Arachne' that offers a profound metaphor for the act of memory itself and the first poem 'We Must Begin' which is both an invocation to memory and an invitation for the reader to trace the poet's inner world through its labyrinths, each poem in the book is distinctly mapped in place and time. Life's journey begins at Manjadithara, 1973 in the poem 'In Amma's Arms' and traverses sixty-one poems to arrive at the last poem in the book, 'The Lone

Petrel' at Ambalamukku, Thiruvanathapuram in 2019. Every poem, one realizes, is a testimony to experience or at least an ode to it, for memory itself is tricky ground and the act of reconstruction is also an intimate act of creation. Memory that posits to be a recollection of the past or a gathering of being in time is also a manifestation of time in being so that an act of memory becomes, equally, an act of narrativizing the self at a moment of time.

In Somarajan's case, the power of his poems stems not only from the deep reflections of his thoughtful and attentive self but also from the unique perception of time that he participates in. His "armchair adventure" as he chooses to call his poetry is built to the rhythm of an alternate temporal logic that privileges depth, density and circularity. Time and place, in his poetry, do not simply constitute a frame within which events occur or are remembered to have occurred but become characters themselves, transformed through the roles that they play. The poems 'The Black Trunk I' (Sainik School, 1984) and 'The Black Trunk II' (Sainik School, 1991) for instance, tenderly bring alive the emotional world of a young boy through a remarkable metaphoric digest of the years spent in school. The black metal trunk is, to the child's eyes, a lie to begin with – a plain metal trunk painted black. The next seven years are built upon this lie and once the lie has been lived to its truth, it is time to falsify it again. This black metal trunk "has given a taste of home/ to a lonely boy, when it could./ Now, it's going home." The idea of home is unsettled with each line till the child is "stunned, orphaned again".

It is worthwhile to examine Somarajan's syntax and admire it for both its studied connotative inwardness and its lush denotative significations. His language is richly interleaved with metaphors and at the centre of every poem shines a luminous metaphoric soul. In 'Kanchenjunga', the poet is a surgeon, a word is a scalpel and the crisp air, a bullet making its way through ether. In 'Incandescent Bulb', memory is a bright bulb staring too long at which numbs the eyes of the mind. 'Concealing Happiness' conjures the word as a firefly whose light must be crushed to bereave it of magic or as some grape which has to be squeezed dry to be made prosaic. Here, "Happiness is a flicker, a derelict checkpoint,/a minor speed-bump." 'Ode to a Pineapple' describes the pineapple's rind as a "cloak of secrecy" and "the blueprint of an assault". In 'Leaving Bangalore', "the city is prose masquerading as poetry". Nowhere, however, is Somrajan more poignant than in describing the act of poetry itself. In 'Remembering Rumi' he says, "Poetry begins where clamour ends." Again, "Your most ambitious poem is silence. Master it." In 'Time: Many Eyes', the poet writes, "Poetry is subterfuge – /the craft lies and deceives./ It's always way above or below, the language of grey,/ neither here nor there – speaking in third person."

In his lecture, 'A Poet's Creed', Borges says:

I have toyed with an idea—the idea that although a man's life is compounded of thousands and thousands of moments and days, those many instants and those many days may be reduced to a single one: the moment when a man knows who he is, when he sees himself face to face.

Across the poems in *First Contact*, one meets similar revelations when a wealth of observation and experience is densely packed into one extraordinary line. The task that the poet has set before himself – to foray into what he understands as the nebulous and endangered zone of memory, is both immense and extraordinary and poetry that responds to it must be far from dilettantism. Revisiting four and a half decades of his life against the grim challenges of his neuromuscular disorder, Somarajan's poetry is an act of existential activism. Though his ordering of life here follows chronology, one realizes that the inner life that the poet describes is a fractal where every part is embedded in the whole and every whole mirrors the part. The self that matures under the chronological ordering of years defies linearity, growing as a palimpsest of all his former selves. Memory, as these poems amply justify, is deeply rooted in forgetting and only from the vantage point of one can the other be understood with any degree of clarity. It is under the threat of forgetting and dissolution that the volition of memory is most consciously activated. But even then, memory is not independent of time. Compounded under the force of time's urgency, the time of recollection is vitally significant to both memory and poetry in the Wordsworthian sense. "The horrors and joys I experienced daily, it did set free – so that I may exist, live further," writes Somarajan.

In travelling through *First Contact*, the reader cannot but feel looming over page after page, the terse thematic triangle of Shakespeare's sonnets where time, love and poetry continually chase each other. Only, on Somarajan's canvas, love is replaced with memory. Time threatens to disfigure memory, memory challenges by reconstructing time and this entire performance is enacted through poetry. Poetry, thus, becomes a performative act of narration of the self, of the world, of time and of the dissonance between all three. It makes up for loss as it constantly imagines new ways to connect with the world. To the desolation of the void in both the world and in the self, poetry offers language and succour. It is an act of charting the void within and that of filling it with meaning. It is a choice to record and imaginatively reclaim all that has drifted away, realizing with gratitude, as Somarajan says, that poetry is a privilege, a thanksgiving for the right to life.

In A Burning Tongue: Soz's *Masculinity Digs a Grave over My Body*

Examining the paradoxical place of the body in poststructuralist critical theory, Jay Prosser, in *Second Skins*, writes, "A glance at any number of new titles shows bodies are everywhere in contemporary cultural theory; yet the paradox of theory's expatiation upon bodies is that it works not to fill in that blind spot so much as to enlarge it." Conversations on embodiment, one will observe, are the least forthcoming in our culture. As Prosser insists, "Materiality is our subject, but the body is not our object. The body is rather our route to analyzing power, technology, discourse, language." And, indeed, though the body as signifier has been discussed threadbare in critical discourse, discussions of lived experiences of embodiment in the face of abuse, violence, disability, pregnancy, pathology, dysphoria, etc. have remained marginal by far. Bodies, one realizes, are as diverse and heterogenous as individuals are, and the unique truth of one's corporeality must be lived out and through every moment of each day. However, embodiment, it will be admitted, does not exist in vacuum but is experienced, interpreted, defined, glorified, stigmatized, contested and challenged within a social, cultural and political context with the personal narrative of the body being often, at odds, with its public narrative. *Masculinity Digs a Grave over My Body* (Red River, 2018), a slender collection of twenty-two extremely powerful, dissident, and confessional poems by Soz, is a book that attempts to place the body and the plethora of cultural discourses surrounding it, at the centre of its poetic universe, and articulates, through the confessions of its particular embodiment, burning questions about the status of the body in mainstream socio-cultural narratives.

Even a cursory glance at these poems will establish Soz's corporeal identity for the reader. As the poems and the title of the collection amply illustrate, the voice behind them is that of a transwoman – whose biologically-assigned masculinity militates against her feminine understanding and experience of her body as female. Unable to culturally identify with the man her body was meant to be, or biologically experience herself as the woman that she intensely identifies with, Soz considers herself to be " a lie/ born out of my mother's womb." Negotiating this difficult embodiment and scarred with the need to conform to the gender binary, her poems are intimate documents of her suffering, angst, rage and the existential necessity to belong in the face of this overwhelming betrayal by the body. In the poem, 'confession I the secret of every 'body', Soz writes:

my mother does not know I am wearing her sari tonight, that my body which does not find a home being a man or a woman, often changes sides on this binary to feel at ease with myself. at the prayers held after my grandfather's death, the audience sat in two groups. i only wanted to sit in between because on the spectrum of gender I fail to find a spot to occupy. so I went and sat with my grandmother instead, holding her as her grief did not come out as tears and the audience was killing her with a façade of pain they did not feel but kept up.

Sex and gender, though often experienced as one seamless category or as logical extensions of one another, are two different conceptual entities with widely divergent expressions. While sex refers to the biological or anatomical dimension of being a male or a female, gender refers to the psychological, social and cultural aspects of being a man or a woman. When sex and gender refuse to align with each other and a case of gender incongruence is experienced, it is understood as dysphoria. Dysphoria, in general, refers to an uneasiness or dissatisfaction with something. Gender dysphoria, particularly refers to the experience of having a psychological and emotional identity that does not correspond to one's biological sex. In Soz's case, dysphoria is the experience of being born male but feeling a psychological and emotional identity as female. This incongruity can be the source of deep and ongoing discomfort, both physically and psychologically, and the trauma of the experience is further compounded by socio-cultural stigmatization of the phenomenon. In Soz's poems, one comes across the confession of the inability to speak about the body's secrets to even her own mother, that most intimate of companions with whom the experience of embodiment is first shared. In 'i'm not my mother's daughter', the poet writes:

> in this country,
> only women have fought
> for inheritance rights.
> i too will fight

to inherit my mother's saris
knowing
i am not her daughter,
knowing
she is my mother.

The body, as Soz's poems, present, is a complex and difficult terrain to transact. The most unique and private of referents for being and the self, the body, one discovers, is anything but personal. It is a site subject to relentless socio-cultural scrutiny, socialization, policing and interpretation, with the result that it can only be a liability to forever account for. In 'a letter to my closet', for instance, Soz says:

since i was born
i was born in
this body along with its cracks,
along with its crevices.
this body has only been a burden.
cover it, they said.
close it, they said.
shut it, they said.
covered it, closed it, shut it.

The most immediate of homes, of anchors and of places, the dysphoric body fails to home its self. Masculine in its appearance and feminine in its experience, the body is a house divided against itself, so much so, that in 'firaaq', the poet states:

my skin
cannot be in a relationship
with itself.
it will have to be peeled
and separated for that.

Richly metaphoric, movingly eloquent in their expression of grief, and powerfully cognizant of the social injustice that inheres within cultural endorsements of gender ideas, these poems, as Mark Greene writes in his Introduction to the book, are "the work of someone who is still constructing who they are. As such, what Soz writes is raw, sexual, challenging and deeply self-referential. It is a mirror searching for courage, seeking the curve of the feminine along the silhouette of the masculine, searching for the pieces of fragmented identity among the errors and failings of being male and female." In a world, where masculinity is power, these poems reflect the underside of the experience of being considered a male and the sacrifices that the construction of masculinity demands. In 'there is no god, only the state', for instance, the poet states:

masculinity is demanding its due ego. my tears are not respected, and so pleasure does not walk into my body. it stays on the door as a thief, at least until the state leaves. histories which have guarded the entrances to my body are meeting histories guarding another's. pleasure waits and waits but the state stays. Pleasure leaves a letter to my tongue, 'i wanted to meet you but you were busy.'

Again, in 'a love letter to masculinity', Soz writes:
dear masculinity,
if I give you away before birth
i can save my tears
and
the expense for your last rites.

The poem, 'on paper, a home means nothing', is, perhaps, one of the most powerful and memorable poems in the collection, drawing attention to the fragility of home for the marginal, to its inadequacy, its vulnerability, its deferral and the impossibility, as a whole, of ever finding and keeping it:

> what of violence
> which is another word
> for home,
> unnamed violence
> like unnamed files
> stored on the desktop
> we do not delete,
> unquestioned violence
> like unquestioned silence
> that waits to be a ceiling
> that needs to be broken
> to see through
> the fractured walls
> we do not notice, the leakages
> we do not repair,
> unless the water leaks…

Emphasizing night as the only time when the dysphoric body, free from cultural constraints, can be experienced as itself, and female clothes as the only home that it can possibly have out of its own divided skin, these poems make a strong case for the poignant liminality of queer space and time, and the necessity of bringing such discourses into the cultural mainstream. Refusing to resort to capital letters at all in valourization of her marginal identity, using images drawn from the natural world to establish the naturalness of gender fluidity and consistently urging the need to re-examine the efficacy of the binary gender model, these are poems that, indeed, as the pen-name of their creator, Soz, indicates, are on fire, and need to be read by the world at large so that their militant voice may seep deep and spread far.

In *Ten Windows: How Great Poems Transform the World*, Jane Hirshfield writes, "Any art able to move us holds somewhere within it both the courage and the knowledge of tears." Poetry, being innumerable things in itself, is also an attempt to heal through cathartic self-expression. Catharsis in poetry comes, above all, from discovering the right tongue for our most unsettling experiences and from putting into exact and satisfactory words a knowledge that is particular, subjective, idiosyncratic and marginal. The search for the right words, the right expression, the right tongue is seldom easy. It rarely comes without great agonizing and critical self-scrutiny but once it does, the poem becomes a space for healing not just the writing-self but every consciousness that pauses to read and reflect in it. The poems of Soz, every reader will admit, constitute just such a space. While they certainly empower the poet through the agency of narrativizing the journey towards her identity, they also constitute a potent space for healing from the experience of incongruence between the self and the world. And to conclude with Hirshfield's words:

> They bring hope. They bring community, inscribing into our thirst for connection poetry's particular, compassionate compact, the inseparability of our own lives and the lives of others, of all that exists. They bring tears. And they promise that these are banquet recognitions we may enter and eat of, if we look and feel through even the briefest poem's eyes.

Cartograph of Identity: Anita Nahal's *What's Wrong With Us Kali Women?*

To begin with, the title *What's Wrong With Us Kali Women?* (Kelsay Books, 2021) nudges you. Here you are, struggling to keep the show going, attempting laboriously to conceal all ripples upon life's surface, trying hard to pretend everything is just the way you have always wished it to be, and then comes along this book that begins its narrative with the presumption of 'something wrong' at the heart of your existence. You feel both understood and betrayed. The book, you have easily surmised, is about you. Aren't you a woman living in and through *Kaliyug*? You closely inspect the four women on the inky blue cover. One of them is looking at a child in her arms, two of them have their gazes fixed elsewhere while the fourth has taken off her sunglasses to stare you straight in the eye – confident and provocative. The first three women, you concede, bear some kinship with you. Like them, you are caught up in roles that have often led you away from yourself. The fourth woman's scrutiny, however, disturbs you a little, amplifying the sense of 'wrong' that the title bespeaks. Feeling both attracted and a trifle insecure, you decide to take the plunge and squarely confront whatever the ensuing pages will reveal.

The journey into the seventy prose poems that the book holds, is unstoppable once it begins. The thoughtful analysis, critical self-evaluation, searing honesty and indomitable optimism of these poems immediately disarm the reader. In the face of such unswerving self-revelation, the most stubborn pretences melt away. One returns, time and again, to the title poem with which the book begins:

> There's nothing wrong. Nothing wrong. That's your fear labelling us. We are the *Kali* women. And all other female, male, androgynous gods. We don't distinguish. We seek. We learn. Comprehend. Embrace. We are the *Kali* women. In the forefront, striding and yes, strutting our stuff too.

The adjective 'Kali' in the title begins to take on new meanings now. These are poems not merely about the new women of the *Kaliyug* who are leaving orthodox traditions behind to explore new spaces and potentialities but also, about women who are honest and bold enough to take on the spirit of the goddess Kali. Kali women, as the book emphasizes, must nurture strength not merely as ambition but for survival and existence in an abusive, discriminating world. Above all, these are poems about taking heart and pride in the intrinsic flamboyance and sheer possibilities of womanhood. In '*Maryada* and modern *Draupadi*' Nahal writes:

> I want to feel special when I lay down, unforgettable
> So, I chose to be me. A woman. Earthy and sensual.

Located within the Indian American diaspora space, Nahal's third collection of poems is, among other things, an intimate account of a female, first-generation, Indian immigrant's challenging home-making in and between cultures and continents. Choosing to settle in America following a traumatic marital relationship in India, many of the poems are poignant snapshots of the poet's own experiences in life – the attempt to negotiate a stressful conjugal relationship, boarding the plane to America with her little son, battling ethnic and gender stereotypes in the new land, raising her son as a single parent, finding meaning in her incessant struggles, anchoring her being and those of others around her in hope, dissent and faith, and finally, acquiring the maturity, confidence and emotional distance to talk matter-of-factly about each of these difficult episodes in poetry. None of these experiences, the reader will realize, has been easy. In 'Sleepless Nights', for instance, the poet says:

I try to reassure the pawns and the elephants that the mounts are being tended to, but one game of chess gives me away. I don my royal clothes and try to appear majestic as I stride out to allay fears of my ailing armies, but sleepless nights don't let go. Don't let go and hold on to the reigns like lonely seaweeds in a forgotten marsh. And the brittle leaves of the now overlooked storm have pressed dried as book marks in my prenatal novel.

While memories of her childhood in India, surface from time to time in Nahal's poetry and she acknowledges her "debt to two lands" ('Paying my debt to two lands'), there is no hyphenation in her emotional identity. Her native country having betrayed her, she can never belong to it again, except in name. "To the place where I was born but felt no allegiance. Its people, my people, gave me no refuge," she states in 'Claustrophobia'. Home, for her, lies essentially and undoubtedly in America, the land she voluntarily claimed for a new beginning. She puts it succinctly in 'Tequila and spice memories':

From New Delhi to America holding my son's

little hand, I mapped, and I trekked. Reels and reels of happenings, instances, episodes, moments that I rolled on my fingertips, even pleated, and clutched and embraced. Owned. Professed. Conceded. Some, I disputed. And laid the admitted neatly, one on top of another like my Indian shawls and saris in cedarwood drawers I bought at flea markets in Virginia suburbs. Mustiness of spices and Fall leaves mingled to create original, unmarked fragrances, new retentions. Every now and then, I recline observing life as I have a couple of tequila shots and hold my tongue on the stories I tell.

The new land is no utopia, of course, and the poet is candid about the injustices and tests that America puts its non-white migrants through. 'How easy it is for a Black life to be taken', for instance, documents the violation and easy expendability of black lives in the US:

How easy it is for a Black life to be taken. Castile, Floyd, Garner, Blake, Brown, Rice, Bland, Gray, Martin, Arbery, Taylor, Till. Not just any names. They were living. Someone's loved ones. Living. Alive. Stolen. Purloined. How easy it is for a Black life to be taken.

In 'You are an immigrant too', the poet offers a confident and balanced self-assessment of her legitimate identity as an American in the multicultural American space:

So, please don't ask where I am from unless your lineage is clear gel, as chained, shackled, sardined, non-resident alien are not words just stamped on my forehead. Unless amnesia is a non-existent word in your heritage dictionary. And then, there was once upon a time, a time engineered for the flow of forced horse-shoe blue bloods, and pedigrees who turned amnesiac soon after. I left the blue blood of my pedigree sitting lonely at erstwhile airport terminal when I arrived disapproved and stamped, fresh off the boat.

These lines, to me, are strongly reminiscent of Bharati Mukherjee's oft-quoted line from her essay 'Two Ways to Belong in America' - "America spoke to me—I married it—I embraced the demotion from expatriate aristocrat to immigrant nobody, surrendering those thousands of years of 'pure culture', the *saris*, the delightfully accented English." For Nahal too, America is her chosen home where she struggles to make space for her multiple identities – immigrant, ethnic, gender, professional, non/marital, maternal, cultural, sexual, gerontological and creative. There is no one way of being anything in the world and her American space offers her the liberty to explore possibilities and choices that allow her to lead life on her own terms. 'Babylon, my sinful dance muse', for instance, describes a club that becomes a valuable space of self-expression for the poet:

My sinful love, Babylon with low lights, hookahs and cigars, Go-Go bands, DJ and club music, food and spirits plenty. And the dance floor was like my bed that I could make love on with the man of my fantasies without any *desi* pointing a finger. *"Hey, you...have you gone mad! A woman with a grown-up son, dancing in mini dresses late at night, drinking booze in those cheesy American clubs instead of prostrating before Hindu Gods praying for peaceful old age!"* Babylon, thank you, for being my sinful dance muse.

However, prejudices and prescriptions from her native culture are not entirely absent in the new world. They resurface from time to time in the form of public opinion, custom or ritualistic proscription, leading the poet to question her epistemological anchoring anew on each of these occasions. The poignant poem 'And then the pundit asked for my son's father's family name', deftly articulates the pain of a single mother whose brave and tumultuous voyage to raise a child in America is belittled in one single moment when the pundit asks for the name of the non-parenting father:

> I thought I'd planned it to a T, all the intricate details. Ceremonies like a mapper chalked out. But for silly validation, forgot the paternal family name is still sought after. As a couple walks seven times around the sacred wedding fire, the pundit asks the boy for his father's name. Patriarchal societies still perpetuated.

At a deeper and more existential level, home, for Nahal is constituted by her son whose significant presence watermarks all her writing and of whom, we receive touching snippets in the poems both in this volume and in her second collection, *Hey, Spilt milk is spilt, nothing else* (2018). A close reading of Nahal's poetry reveals that her survival owes itself not only to Gods, destiny, lands, her own tenacity, and her indomitable, phoenix-like spirit, but also to the strength she derives from her son with whom she shares and wishes to share an unbreakable mother-son-soulmate bond from life to life. In her poem, 'Why I usually cry in the shower,' whose last lines are as touching and memorable as Ezekiel's famed 'Night of the Scorpion', the poet pours her deepest tears to God in an unspoken prayer that always seems to be on her lips:

> After my tears have been fully pulled out, drained, syphoned, and dried, then I become tranquil, and gratefulness fills my heart. Not everyone has everything. If I have to go through the same all over, in another life, I'll

accept it as long as in each timeframe my child isborn to me again.

In poem after poem, Nahal emphatically stands up for the strength of single motherhood through the intensity of feminist determination and humanist resolve, triumphantly articulated in, 'Fallacy of a single immigrant mom,'

Folks only saw the tip above the waters for mom and son. We were like Maya Angelou's oil wells were pumping in our living room despite first furniture being hand-me-downs. I am a single, immigrant, pleased, grateful mom. And that's no fallacy.

Distinctly marking Nahal's poems are also ruminations on the lives of women and all humans in general, the stereotypes and violence that are rampant in both the East and the West, the pandemic and the large-scale human losses that it has entailed, and the urgent need to rethink the relationship between the human and the non-human worlds. She urges her readers to ponder over a plethora of injustices such as poverty, skin colour, ageism, ills of democracy, even debunking human narcissism ('Smooth operators', 'Hard: Us, animals and the aliens', 'Family blood') among others and in doing so clearly establishes her humanist approach to life, animals and also alien life. She questions our very existence ('Ancient creation') and concludes that the mysteries of life will remain as these are and like alchemists we can only keep moving, creating, revising and revisiting these essentially unknowable phenomena.

What animates this collection, above all, is the sense of creating something new out of the experiences that life has brought one's way. At the centre of these poems stands tall, a speaker who refuses to be at the receiving end of things and has the determination, ability, skill, creativity and courage to forge slowly from what is received, all that is desired. Each poem in the volume maps a steady journey into a self that grows, matures, and strengthens with every experience till it realizes, in itself, its greatest and worthiest asset. Such wisdom does not come from the repudiation or denial of any aspect of life or feeling and Nahal's consistent reflective practice involves the bringing and interrogating of every experience on poetry's table for exploration and illumination. The present, for Nahal, can only be built by acknowledging the past and the future shall be paved only through determined negotiation with the present. There will be demons, spilt milk and Judases. The journey into an enlightened and expanded subjectivity may, often, be solitary and loveless. But one's true allegiance will always be to the self and to the treasures it holds deep within it.

Feminist, rational, confessional and empathetic, *What's Wrong With Us Kali Women?* is a compelling creative act of cartographing an empowered selfhood in which every reader will be drawn to participate. Leading you to confront and accept your own fissures, it will leave you feeling saner and stronger. Having entered into a dialogue with these poems, the cover speaks to you now in distinct ways. Here are a host of stereotypes effectively demolished. The woman with the child in her arms stands, perhaps, for maternal feminism and also the strength and optimism of single motherhood. The professional-looking woman and the older woman on the right who have their gazes elsewhere, exude a calm confidence that bespeaks a Kintsugi-like approach to life's travails. The details of facial expression, posture and clothing, seem to have all been carefully constructed to convey questions and meanings of the myriad stages and ages of a woman's journey from a lover, wife, mother, a professional woman, a grandmother - all denoting the quintessential Kali woman who knows how to repair the fractures of life in the Japanese way, with gold. Having recognized these women for aspects of yourself and having bared your own soul to them, when you finally shut the book, you establish a deep bond with the fourth mysterious and alluring woman at the centre of the cover. Confidently confronting her gaze, you smile back, knowing a friend has been found in the self forever.

On the Grave Business of Poetry: GJV Prasad's *This World of Mine: Selected Poems*

Let us begin with the book's title. *This World of Mine* (Hawakal Publishers, 2021) – says GJV Prasad and the deliberate use of the pronoun 'this' immediately makes the 'world' objective and shared with the reader, at least through signification. This idea then, of the world being shared, lessens the force of the possessive pronoun 'mine', establishing that this said world's contours are neither eccentric nor idiosyncratic but very much identifiable and relatable. And yet, the 'mine' retains its presence and cannot be dismissed completely. There is no denying the poet's claim to this world. For better or worse, this is the place that he inhabits and chooses to be inhabited by.

Look closer at the book's cover and the green will draw you in – light, buoyant, the colour of regeneration and peace. What strikes you forcefully, however, is the quiet owl scrutinizing your gaze. The owl's presence warns you that this world is going to be dark and it is up to you to stay or leave. You trust its wisdom and decide to stay. In the fifty poems that follow, you are stirred to look at this world that you share with the poet, anew. It is not as if you never saw this before but refracted through GJV Prasad's idealism, realism, humour – grim and often sardonic, his acuity, reflection and honest acquiescence, the shadowy world becomes compellingly concrete. You are grateful that you chose to stay and be showed around this world that you might never have discovered on your own.

Prasad's first book of poems, *In Delhi without a Visa* was published to critical success in 1996. *This World of Mine: Selected Poems* is his second poetry collection that makes its appearance after nearly twenty-five years. Given the committed nature of Prasad's art, this long silence is difficult to explain. In 'Poetry', he writes:

> Why does poetry make so much sense to me
> When I never know what the poets mean
> Why does poetry give me so much energy
> When it takes so much effort to read

To anyone, even summarily acquainted with Prasad's critical acumen and towering stature as a critic, these lines are bound to be baffling. And yet, at a deeper level, they do not only bear themselves out but also help explain the poet's ambiguous relationship with poetry. Note the delicate opposition of the words 'mean' and 'sense' as also, of the words 'energy' and 'effort'. Since poetry means so much, it must be well-weighed. The trained linguist that Prasad is, he deftly plays with the various registers of a word, trapezing across to suit his fancy as well as to beguile the reader.

The poems in this collection are unapologetically political. Whether it is fanaticism, fundamentalism, sexism, communalism, postcolonialism, Marxism, feminism, or more – Prasad will not shy away. He will tell you the truth exactly as he sees it, sans metaphor, sans slant, and sans any personal *ism*, amply exemplifying that this world in all its paradoxes and ambiguities, is truly 'his' and there is no turning his back upon this responsibility for it. In 'The View', the golden sunset that alchemizes the poet can hardly animate the twig-picking old man. "What's so special Babu/ You can't eat it can you?" he says. In 'Her Story', the "lying professors" do not know "how else/ To get a woman student/ Into a relationship". In 'Godhra-Gujarat', all wrongs of Ghazni are duly avenged – "Ten eyes for an eye/ All thirty two for a tooth". In 'Election Strategies: Shining India' "Yearly blood-letting keeps the nation glowing/ The interests in our vote banks growing/ We are the ones who keep India Shining". The responsibility to confront the world as it offers itself is not easy but with the large reserves of wit, sarcasm, and humour that Prasad commands, it is less difficult.

The first meaningfully-placed poem in the collection 'Desperately Seeking India' brings India's diversity, separatism and prejudice admirably together. Here is an emotional acceptance of India's differences and an intellectual admission of failure to surmount them. "I promise/ Never/ To mention India again" says the poet. Inside India, it would be impossible to make an appeal to or for India. So, is unity impossible? The answer is found in 'behold the dark', a poem written for the post-atom bomb world in which physical light become the reason for material darkness and moral luminosity. Prasad writes, "perhaps/ there is a lesson in the dark/ you hold hands/ when you can't see/ with people/ you don't know/ and come together as a world."

But the most riveting political poems in this collection are those that quietly take up the feminist cause. In 'Hey Ram' (a title that conjures both Ram and Gandhi), the husband is "A good family man but better on a committee". In 'Draupadi Said', Draupadi regrets asking Krishna for help, insisting that she had wanted not clothes but "summary, summary justice" and concludes, "I was a fool/ To expect such - / Anything was too much - / From men or Gods". The three poems in the Sati series, placed in historical chronology, throw different lights on the idea of the Sati and showcase, perhaps, Prasad's humour at the grimmest. In Sati I, the funeral pyre is a tragic choice for the widow to end a more tragic and choiceless life. In Sati 2 and 3, there are parallel accounts of Roop Kanwar's tragic burning with Sati 2 documenting the dynamic economics of religion and Sati 3, the façade of it along with the critique of a disconnected diasporic ideology. In 'Edible Woman' (with deliberate resonances of Atwood), the woman, in a fervour of hyperbolic romantic love, becomes to the male lover, every conceivable Indian culinary delicacy - "I mean to say I can snack/ On you any time/ And time and again". In a country where rape is a regular headline, Prasad sardonically points out how even the basic equation of romance is flawed.

JNU which remains an indispensable part of the poet's identity, features prominently in the collection in its myriad flavours in poems like 'JNU', 'How Brown was My Campus', 'Two Writers at JNU', and 'First Class in Room 016'. Personal poems like the Family poems, 'Kai Visiri', 'Ishwar Natarajan' and 'This was Nattu' reveal the softer side of the poet's mind, where emotion gently vanquishes intellect. However, for the greater part of the collection, Prasad's sparkling wit dominates, rising at the service of both clarification and satire. Ruminating on the history of the Taj Mahal in 'where did the masons go', he comments, "love was a grave business/ in this nation." So is poetry (though one cannot overlook the pointed pun on the word 'grave') and one sincerely hopes that more self-reflective and eye-opening poems from GJV Prasad find their way to our unquenched, awaiting hearts in the days to come.

Meditative Dialogues: Gopal Lahiri's *Alleys are Filled with Future Alphabets: Selected Poems*

In his lecture 'A Poet's Creed' for *The Charles Eliot Norton Lectures* (1967-68), Jorge Luis Borges states:

> I have come to the conclusion (and this conclusion may sound sad) that I no longer believe in expression: I believe only in allusion. After all, what are words? Words are symbols for shared memories. If I use a word, then you should have some experience of what the word stands for. If not, the word means nothing to you. I think we can only allude, we can only try to make the reader imagine. The reader, if he is quick enough, can be satisfied with our merely hinting at something.

At a substantially deep level, Borges' assertion holds true, for memorable poetry seldom leaves us with a graspable meaning that we can hold on to. Poetry's truth is never in the concrete but in what the reader makes of its conscious, orchestrated semantic arrangements. Incantative in spirit, a poem's meaning is incapable of sustaining itself outside its particular linguistic universe. To evoke its meaning each time, the poem as a whole must be conjured and re-conjured. In this repeated calling forth lies, also, the test of good poetry. Hence, Matthew Arnold's *Touchstone*

Method, despite its obvious shortcomings, relied on drawing a yardstick for the evaluation of worthy poetry through the constant and conscious recalling of lines from poems that were indisputably classical. The idea dominating this approach was, obviously, the inseparability in enduring poetry, of expression and meaning, or the integrity of what Borges might call expression as allusion.

This quality of expression as allusion looms large over the universe of Gopal Lahiri's latest collection of poems *Alleys are Filled with Future Alphabets: Selected Poems* (Rubric Publishing, 2021) and is powerfully asserted by its cover-painting 'Uncanny' by poet-academic Jharna Sanyal. The 102 poems in this collection chart diverse and highly idiosyncratic thematic journeys. Divided into seven sections, the telling sub-titles - 'Voyages In', 'Voyages Out', 'Cityscape Silhouettes', 'Macrocosm', 'Haiku Series and Micro Poems', 'Travel Diaries' and 'Pandemic and Resilience' – offer cues for navigating through this densely meditative volume. In his critical essay 'Postface' that concludes the collection, John Thieme remarks:

The poems often deal with transient phenomena – moments in the day; the flight of birds; the minutiae of landscapes and cityscapes – and sharply realized observation lies at their core, but observation is never an end in itself [...] and the imagistic underpinning of Gopal Lahiri's verse consistently questions the possibilities of extracting meaning from both the ephemeral present and the partially remembered past.

However, though these poems deal primarily with the concrete and visible, their method of operation is highly imagist and abstract. Lahiri's strength lies in relentless linguistic exploration and in the frequent clinching of ideas through an incisive turn of phrase. In 'Connection', "The real showstopper is now the drunken breeze", in 'Silvery Lies', "The moonbeams knife through the wall papers" and in 'Right Moment, "An empty night has never/lived up to its expectations".

Deep introspection is a defining characteristic of Lahiri's oeuvre. His poetic practice bespeaks an intrinsic dissatisfaction with appearance, evidence and geometry. What intrigues him is the ungraspable, self-militating and unnegotiable essence of things. There is a rampant desire in his poems to unpack the familiar patterns of the world through conscious linguistic reconstructions that border, sharply, on the metaphorical. The canvas of his poetry is the world around him but the focus is relentlessly on the reflection of this world in his own subjectivity. Thus, Lahiri's poems, though they engage in sustained dialogues with the world, are not realist in the conventional sense of the word. In 'City of Joy', for instance, "The trees turn into a series of promises/ syncopated words and sentences/ sublimate into the secret diaries,/ the hustle of the avenues/ swaddle in our lengthy playlist." Here, the trees are both as real and unreal and as denotative and connotative as semantics. In "dialogues are now in/ long queues" from 'Exposure', the idea engenders a stirring ambivalence. Are the dialogues long or is it the very act of engagement in dialogue that is queued up or are both meanings employed in conjoinment?

In her 'Preamble' to the collection, Sharmila Ray remarks:

Reality for Lahiri is sacred in itself not a springboard to reportage or an obstacle. The physical is the spiritual in the sense it voices human heart beats, dilation, respiration which are all part of the cosmos. The capacity to expand a fleeting experience into dense and complex, satisfying both instinct and intellect, is an art the poet is very much at home with.

The real and the metaphorical, as Ray rightly observes, constitute the warp and woof of Lahiri's poetic fabric. His meditations are contingent and etched upon a finite moment suspended in time. Temporal consciousness acutely marks these poems, both in the observations of the world and the self. Both despair and hope are temporally framed and hence, a perpetual site of becoming.

Immensely significant to an understanding of the collection is its visual title *Alleys are Filled with Future Alphabets*. Here is a consciousness of marginality and possibility, of darkness and hope. The pointed semantic choice of the graphic word 'alphabets' also speaks for the volume's strong metaliterary faith in poetry as pathway and destination. Whatever the moment might bring, the map of poetry is potent enough to lead the poet and reader beyond prevarication and into wisdom. Meditative, self-reflexive, exploratory and characterized by an intense linguistic searching, these are poems that will lead readers to think anew about their everyday world and the ways in which they inhabit it.

Unwombing the Mind: Kala Ramesh's *the forest I know*

"I want to be a river with the luxury of being myself, minus regret."

(Kala Ramesh, 'Baggage')

How does a woman attempt to find herself? Her life having been made over to relationships, duties, responsibilities and obligations that she cannot turn away from, how does she respond to the gnawing hunger of her own heart for self-companionship, self-understanding and self-emancipation?

Were women to court binaries of thought, a mode of choice and action would be easy. It might be possible then to s/elect liberation over bondage, joy over suffering, and the self over the other. One could, in such circumstances, choose to travel by roads marked, known, and well-mapped; be unburdened by choices made; and find fellowship throughout the journey.

As things stand, however, the process of women finding themselves, even when they know where to search, is seldom to be learned from a readymade manual or handbook. The experiences of other women who have lived similar lives can and does serve as a powerful searchlight in the expedition but even then, the dialectics of the search, its rationale, and the evaluation of the measure of its success or failure have to be worked out by the individual journeywoman alone.

Kala Ramesh's *the forest i know: a gathering of tanka verses* (Harper Collins, 2021) is a record of one such courageous journey. The metaphor of the forest has often been used by used by women to symbolize the life of the mind. With its associations of density, darkness, creativity and mystery, the forest constitutes a fertile and unmapped space of desire, discovery, negotiation and epiphany.

Ramesh's exploration, as her dedication establishes, is a journey towards "inward flowering". This flowering of the mind, soul or the spirit, however, cannot be accomplished without negotiating with the terrain of her outer world. The poet must relive every significant interaction and episode of her life in order to gather the pieces of herself lost or shred during such encounters. The moments of jubilation, too, must be recapitulated in order to establish the domain of the self in positive terms of empowerment.

Thus, begins a series of poignant ruminations and reflections with the sole object of mapping the journeywoman's distinct and unknown path through childhood, adolescence, adulthood, marriage, motherhood and old age in the six sections of the book evocatively titled 'maya', 'backyard well', 'pellets of desire', 'within and without', 'tanka doha' and 'oneness'. These material and socio-cultural transitions of the body and life-cycle are, each, accompanied by their own sets of migrations – physical and psychological, role-expectations, and the yearnings of selfhood. There is, also, the perpetual disconnect, the inability to fully insert the self into the situation, and an aching aftertaste of unfulfillment and loss:

> having to wear
> several masks in life –
> if only I could
> drift away between scenes
> like a dragonfly

Memory rules the psyche of the collection, becoming the scaffold for most of these poems to register their presence in the world. And yet, this memory, far from the naïve recalling of the past, offers a superior and critical insight into the events that it narrates, opening doors for greater connection, clarity and peace:

> the red dot
> on my forehead
> binds me
> to a man
> who's in his own orbit
> parading
> the so-called equality
> with iron bars concealed…
> this urban woman lives
> in her dreams

Side by side with memory there operates in this collection an insistent awareness of life's cyclical motion – the daughter as mother, the young as old, the receiver as giver and the victor as victim. In 'Vratham', she outlines the legacy of the Ekadashi fast that her grandmother had devoutly observed all her life and whose observance by older women, she as a young girl, had taken for granted. Becoming an adult, however, had led to a judicious questioning of rituals and the hold of tradition on her has declined:

> I've been a mother now for decades… habits and

belief systems change with each generation. The ekadashi fast, now relegated to the past, is one of those stories I'll tell my grandchildren.

Such cyclical consciousness is also fed into these poems by their espousal of and alert responsiveness to the subtle and varied rhythms of the natural world. For Ramesh, the vital world of nature becomes a crucial index for understanding individual experiences and a valuable yardstick for measuring the worth of human values. In 'Azadi', for instance, she writes:

> a million
> daydreams get buried
> at sundown
> both pariah and non-pariah
> walk the fallen leaf path

Pivotal to these poems is a strong and nourishing womanist spirit expressing itself in the pregnant style of the tanka, a form that allows both precision and freedom in its brevity and its capacity to project a thematically sustained narrative with leaps of space, thought, temporality and image. The distilled and aphoristic content of the tanka sans break or punctuation bespeaks a tradition of seamless and potent blending of the personal with the public and Ramesh powerfully establishes her kinship with this tradition by bringing her individual life as a woman in close communion with the socialscape and the omnipresent landscape of nature through memorably sharp images. Note how in 'On Slippery Ground', she etches the experiences of connection in motherhood through wide-ranging ecological metaphors:

> learning to swim
> I'm told you'll know it for life

once you learn...
was it a different me then
in my mother's womb
deep roots
ground the sacred fig tree –
my third trimester
I caress my stomach
... this navel connection

the forest i know begins with 'garbha' – the womb and in giving birth to the essential "storylines" that chart the poet's lived experience and identity, the womb becomes a companion metaphor of the forest – a space of protection, liberation and unmapped redefinition for not just the poet-creator but for every reader who allows herself to enter the book's forest, fragrant with its promise of regeneration.

Championing an Identity sans Signifiers: Kalki Subramaniam's *We are Not the Others: Reflections of a Transgender Artivist*

"I too stand
in the thick of the battle field
destroying stupidity
and defeating
the emasculated,
let us celebrate life,
come."
(Kalki Subramaniam, 'Arise, My Precious')

Kalki Subramaniam's latest collection *We are Not the Others: Reflections of a Transgender Artivist* (Notion Press, 2021) published by Notion Press this June, is a book that will leave your heart open for ever. An honest, unapologetic, and fiery narrative of a transgender's lived experience presented through poetry, prose and through deeply figurative and unsettling illustrations by the talented writer herself, here is writing that takes the heart by storm, wreaks havoc on our complacencies, upsets the neat and futile categories of definitions that have been drilled into us through a prolonged process of socialization, and liberates us by the overwhelming strength of its optimism.

Artist, activist, poet, actor, and writer, Kalki powerfully places her transgender identity at the centre of her rich and multifarious work. Founder of Sahodari Foundation, an organization that works for the social, political, and economic empowerment of transgender people in India through various creative projects, Kalki combines art and activism with a commitment that is not just intellectual or social but defiantly humanist. One of the most prominent voices in the LGBTQI+ community of India, she is well-known for championing the recognition of the legal rights of transgender people which resulted in the historic 2014 verdict of the Supreme Court of India whereby the rights of the transgender community as the third gender were recognized not merely as 'a social or medical issue but a human rights issue'. Widely awarded for her social work, art, film performance, and literary contributions, Kalki continues to be an inspiration both within the transgender community and beyond it. Her poems, as N. Elango writes in his *Foreword* to the collection, are "clarion calls, not only to the LGBT community, but for those whosoever seek to break themselves free from the shackles and fetters snapped around them by the hegemonic conspiracy."

Comprising sixteen poems, some of which have been translated from the original Tamil by N. Elango, four personal essays, and magnificent quotations and artwork, including the actual handwritten scripts of her Tamil poems, the book takes us into an autobiographical journey of growth, strength and faith through the trauma, angst and painful discrimination that transgenders undergo every day in this country. In her *Author's Notes* to the collection, Kalki writes:

> This book is a bundle of so many of my emotions – joy, pain, anger, fury, distress and hope. Through this book, I tell some parts of my story and that of the others like me. You will hear their voices through me.
>
> Poetry and art give a richness to my life. They give beauty, strength and hope. They heal. I couldn't have survived my tormenting teenage years without them.

Signification, one realizes, is a complex process and often, self-defeating. The complexity of signification stems from the fact that the signified, rather than being an objective presence in the real world, constitutes an abstracted idea of it in our minds. Our ideas, often being entrenched by particularities such as history, society, religion, culture and conditioning, the looming possibilities are that a wrong, erroneous and unwarranted idea may root itself over time into a vindictive stereotype. Around us and across the world, the negative effects of such stereotyping are rampantly visible. Stripped of distinctive individual virtues, identity becomes an allotted story of signification that may have no correspondence to fact. Every human and non-human Other is the victim of just such a process of signification whereby the assumed has offset the actual, and ushered in practices of prejudice, discrimination, hatred and violence. When it comes to people who identify themselves as LGBTQI+, the trauma and suffering that pernicious narratives of signification can produce, is heightened by the fact that there is no appeal to a common truth. The only truth about sex and gender is that which also challenges their greatest fallacy viz. they are binary. Nothing can be farther from biological fact. In *From Transgender to Transhuman*, Martine Rothblatt writes:

... sex in humans is a continuous variable, a complex of phenotypic and genotypic factors as unique as one's fingerprints. While male and female categories are useful to group biological characteristics for medical purposes, these same categories have socially detrimental effects when used outside the field of medicine. Sex should really be the sum of behaviors we call gender—an adjective, not a noun. People should explore genders. When they settle on a set of gender behaviors, the name for that set describes their sex.

Rothblatt insists that the resting point for gender "depends upon the same complex of mental propensities and chance socialization that leads people to adopt one or another career, hobby, or religion." However, in a country like India where sex is, in most quarters, destiny and where patriarchal thought largely reigns, transgenders are routinely judged by society for their bodies, voices, physical appearance, sexual choices and morality, so much so, that the ordinary prerogatives of ordinary people everywhere in the world become for them, exclusive privileges they must fight to earn.

In 'If You Don't Mind', the poet describes how the claim of transwomen like her to womanhood, is continually contested by mainstream society that reserves the right to judge her body as an anomaly, and in a blatant invasion of her privacy, to ceaselessly question her about it. 'Don't Tell That to Me' documents, in the same testing spirit of the irritable receiver, what transgenders receive most from the world – curiosity, sympathy, stares, whispers, questions and requests for blessings as if they were divine in their departure from normative humanity. Kalki writes:

> To you and to
> the million others

> I want to shout
> I am made of
> flesh and blood,
> of fear and hope,
> of joy and pain.
> I am like you
> I am human too.

On the terrain of gender identity, gender affirmation for transwomen is no less traumatic. As far as the socio-cultural binary thinking about gender goes, it is not sufficient for a person to identify as a woman. One must also offer evidence of 'being' one as per mainstream norms of body-type and behaviour. Such socio-cultural determination of questions of ontology does grave injustice to real life by refuting the immense variety of embodied gender experience and imposing a blanket uniformity on the internalization and articulation of womanhood. 'Piece by Piece' that examines gender identity as a process of becoming rather than de facto being, is a poem that talks of the poet's struggle to painstakingly establish her claim as a woman:

> I am not a woman by birth
> I was born as a shattered
> Rubik's cube,
> all my life I worked
> step by step
> to reclaim my honour.
> To correct the wrongs,
> I collected all of me,
> my body, mind and soul
> and put together in patience,
> vouching with perseverance.

> I endured shame and guilt,
> yet I stood strong with grit.

In the heart-wrenching poem 'Nirvaanam', the multi-layered issues surrounding gender – biology, culture, policing and performance – poignantly coalesce. The transwoman's joy in her anklet and her ecstatic dance invite ridicule from the moral police, "those/ who have their manhoods/ hanging about them". The only way for the woman here to "stand my ground/ to prove my womanhood", is through biology:

> with tears rolling down
> I remove my saree.
> In this moment,
> I do not want any Krishna
> to save or rescue me

The act of disrobing is transformed here into an act of agency and defiant transgression. Its complex and potent symbolism is heightened by the mythological subtexts that it skilfully builds, both evoking and rejecting the need of a male God to protect the sham cultural notion of 'honour'. The female body which has historically borne the brunt of violence against women in society now becomes a vital site for the empowered assertion of female identity, beyond the need of patriarchal intervention or safeguard. This is not to say that the element of victimization is absent here but the conscious attempt is to wrest power for the woman against all odds.

'Truth and Lie' documents another painful moment of rejection, this time, in love. In a potential bond of marriage, the poet-speaker's revelation of her real identity as a transwoman, spoils all her conjugal hopes:

"I told you not to out
yourself as a Transwoman.
My parents rejected you,
I need them and
can't reject them,
so I reject you"
you spoke.

This is a culture that, as the poem points out, punishes honesty and will forgive and even welcome inauthenticity at the cost of maintaining its illusions intact. In her prose pieces 'My Perfectly Imperfect Vagina' and 'Will an Indian Man Ever Bring a Trans Woman Home and Say 'Ma, I Love Her'?, Kalki evocatively describes the transwomen's existential necessity to acquire the biological gift of womanhood through sex-reassignment surgeries and society's prejudiced rejection of them as women despite their fierce identification as members of the female sex. In the former essay, she writes:

Women who are 'born women' are gifted with a perfect vagina, they don't have to spend a dime or a rupee to have a perfect one. But our stories, the transwomen's stories are entirely different. Before we did our sex reassignment surgeries, those days whenever we looked down naked, we were ashamed and wanted to pluck it off whatever was hanging there. We loathed it.

The essay throws light on the various experiences of gender dysphoria and the non-seriousness of the government in dealing with it. In poems like 'She' and 'Clap Aloud', Kalki deconstructs the stereotyping of transgenders by establishing their clapping as an act of empowerment and liberation from the misplaced and hypocritical values of society – "Clap aloud/ Thirunangai/ clap aloud!/ Like a crack of thunder/ that shocks the world/ during a great rain,/ clap your hands aloud!" The ability to have both hands free for oneself and for service to humanity becomes a higher form of ethic than the selfish engagements of the workaday world. The act of clapping, thus, becomes an assertion of humanity and of the superior knowledge of identification of the self with the world.

Rothblatt states that the "apartheid of sex" by which we are cast, from the time of our birth, into a sex-type based on our genitals and socialized into a "sex-type-appropriate culture called gender" is extremely detrimental to society. "Freedom of gender is," in her opinion, "therefore, the gateway to a *freedom of form* and to an explosion of human potential. First comes the realization that we are not limited by our gross sexual anatomy. Then comes the awakening that we are not limited by our anatomy at all. The mind is the substance of humanity. Mind is deeper than matter."

Kalki, in her writing, also strongly argues for the evaluation of humans as humans, irrespective of gender. In her prose piece 'A Letter to a Transgender Kid', she attempts to put forward a narrative of androgyny that is gloriously human:

Do remember that there is no complete man or complete woman in this world. If anyone as such existed ever, they can never understand the emotions of the opposite gender. In every man, there is a woman and, in every woman, there is a man. How much of a man is a woman, and how much of a woman is a man is what makes them. Makes us all.

Each piece of writing in *We are Not the Others: Reflections of a Transgender Artivist* deconstructs the idea of transgenders as Others by deconstructing cultural signification and offering an insider's account of their dreams, desires, hopes, pain and suffering that are all too universal and all too human. Challenging the stereotyping of signifiers, these are pieces that vehemently bring home to us the fact that boy/girl/man/woman/first gender/ second gender/third gender are hierarchical categories that we forcefully impose upon human experience with severe injustice and irreparable damage. It is important to acknowledge the diversity of life, of living and of performing humanity across bodies, genders, cultures and sexual orientations. "This book," writes Laura Sherwood, "is essential for all academic institutions and programs working to dismantle dominant narratives or facilitate dialogue around gender beyond the binary." I would like to affirm that this is a work that must be read by everyone who wishes to know, first-hand, of human grit, perseverance, and the human ability to, both, fuel and transcend them through art. Also that, once read, this is a book no reader will be able to permanently disentangle her memory and consciousness from.

Manifestations of Light: Kavita Ezekiel Mendonca's *Light of The Sabbath: Poems about Memories and the sacredness of Light*

All around us, light is ubiquitous. And yet, how much of this light actually penetrates our consciousness? How many times do we, voluntarily, awaken to light, admit its clarity into our souls, are willing to, single-mindedly, pursue its being, and allow ourselves to be unquestioningly transformed by it? Very few of us, we would confess. In fact, the contrary often holds true for light – it is pursued when it is most invisible. Being taken for granted, light's everyday presence around us easily goes unnoticed. It is merely a part of the backdrop, something that, given time and season, must exist. We shrug at its being and move on. However, the moment this privilege is taken away, we feel restless, indignant, wronged.

At an existential level, light manifests itself as a metaphor for many feelings – joy, goodness, contentment, gratitude, love, kinship, hope, faith, and more. Both the world and the spirit's geography are revealed through light. Being indeterminate and evasive by nature, light can always be lost. Being omnipresent, it will always be found, if well-sought. To heighten one's perception to light's fragility and to vest faith in its omnipresence, requires a consciousness that is, to a considerable degree, transcendent. To meditate on light will involve a resolute turning away from the meanness of time, the ingratitude of our days and the world's shape-shifting errors. To elevate such meditations into memorable poetry will call for a resonance to light's luminosity. Kavita Ezekiel Mendonca, as any reader of *Light of The Sabbath* (Chapbook, 2021) will realize, has effectively done them all.

"Growing up, Light was an important subject of conversation in my home – how to read in the best light, how to write with proper lighting, opening the windows and curtains to the morning light, appreciating light in all the various forms of illumination that invigorated one's being. It became something of a sacred consciousness," writes Mendonca in her note 'From the Poet's Desk'. These poems which she describes as "an attempt to discover my Jewish roots, and the meaning and impact my upbringing has in forming my world view and my life today" constitute a compound inquiry on the idea of light on many planes – religious, spiritual, familial, ethical, moral, emotional, and practical. One will notice that I have abstained from using the word 'intellectual' here and rightly so, for Mendonca's poems, in myriad ways, offer the reader a respite from the intellectual. There is no syllogism here, no ratiocination, no point to be enforced by example or argument. There is no conscious linguistic artistry, no posture, and absolutely no irony in her poetry. Here is an intense soul-flowering of the lyric and a spontaneous expression of the profound musings of a soul that is in continuous dialogue with its many temporal selves.

The theme of identity looms large over the collection. Many of the poems here, are attempts to establish a connection not only across her Canadian present and Indian past but also, across generations of her Bene-Israel Jewish community in India. In the poem 'Shipwreck', Mendonca attempts to condense a narrative of the community's arrival on the subcontinent:

> The ship struck a rock
> The ship broke, God's rock stood firm
> It carried my people to a new land
> A different destiny.
> […]
> Settling in nearby villages
> Blending into the landscape
> They pressed the oil, became oil pressers
> Of the local seed, Saturday oil pressers, *Shanwar Telis*, my ancestors
> […]
> I am from the same seed
> […]
> I survive
> Like my ancestors.
> Pressing seeds into verse
> To preserve a story of survival
> Not just on Saturdays.

'Alibaug' is another rich tribute to her ancestors and the simple, pre-industrialized way of life that shall never be recovered again:

> I miss Alibaug
> The flickering lanterns, sleeping on mats, eating from *thalis
> I miss Alibaug

> The hushed whispers between cousins
> I don't know when I can return
> To the land of my ancestors
> The land of the *Shanwartelis*, the Oil pressers

Like her late father, Nissim Ezekiel, Kavita Ezekiel Mendonca's poetry exhibits a keen eye for detail as she attempts to record the world around her as she sees it – with a complete acceptance of its follies and sans rancour. Her chosen subject in this slim collection of twenty-eight poems is, as she puts it, her "Indian-Jewish heritage" and "the warm memories of growing up with the customs and traditions of the culture, faith and personalities of my parents, grandparents, and extended family." Narrativized in these poems are animated recollections of religious celebrations, family visits, love for close relatives and beloved possessions, and the ways in which the past and the present are deeply entwined together. 'The Ballad of Little Ma', for instance, celebrates the love and resilience of the poet's maternal grandmother:

> Little Ma had thirteen children,
> Nine survived, one was my mother,
> The rest were the village that raised me,
> Loving, doting, aunts and uncles,
> Saviors from a strict mother.
> I wondered how Ma's small frame carried
> so many children in her tiny body.
> I carried two, my body not so little as hers.

'China Grass Halwa' pays an affectionate tribute to an aunt whose house had little room and not many belongings but whose heart, in its affection and generosity, was immense. In 'Chain of Events', the poet amusedly traces the whimsical journey of a gold chain across generations till it is finally found in her closet – a heirloom that preserves intact her connection with her lost family. 'Give me Oil in my Lamp' is another heart-warming poem that describes the poet's childhood visits to the synagogue with her paternal grandmother and the way her grandmother would give her a Jewish name, Elizabeth, only in order to sign the receipt for filling oil in the lamp.

Light emerges as a significant trope in these poems in all its metaphoric, symbolic and sensory forms. There is the nostalgic light of cheerful memories, the religious light of the Sabbath, the ritualistic light of the lamp burning in the synagogue, the physical light of the sunrise and twilight, the spiritual light of the Jewish blessing 'Mazel Tov' and the immortal light of the Muse. 'How to light up a poem', for instance, is a metaliterary piece that in ways akin to Ezekiel's 'Poet, Lover, Birdwatcher', metaphorically describes the art of poetic creation. In images that are strongly romantic and ecocentric, Mendonca conjures the gentle art of writing a poem:

> Gently petition the moon for some moonbeams, scatter them gently on the path
> Implore the sun for a ray or two, scatter deliberately along the way
> Ask the trees for shadows and silhouettes, brush the path with shades of these
> Strike up a conversation with the trees, soon there will be a dialogue.

However, the best part of a poem, as Mendonca agrees, is that which cannot consciously be birthed. Certain things have to be left to the mystery and magic of creation. Hence, the poet's advice:

> If after doing all these things you do not manage to light up the poem

> Don't worry, when the light wants to come in,
> It will knock.

However, to say that these poems have totally vanquished the dark would be untrue. Watermarked by the memory of the Holocaust and the large-scale historical deprivation of Jews worldwide, these poems are also acts of, what Saranya Subramaniam in her Foreword to the collection, calls "archival activism". Consider the haunting memory of hunger in 'The last Slice' where the poet, on the verge of throwing the last thin slice of bread into the garbage bin, recalls the hunger of Jewish prisoners:

> Remembered them, the doomed prisoners
> They got no bread, often just crumbs
> The same crumbs, the ones I shook out
> Out of the toaster, to prevent a toaster fire.
> I was not there, but I saw in visions
> Their crumbs with the snow boot marks,
> Should the fallen bread kiss the ground.

By trying to go back in time, place and culture, Mendonca's journey towards understanding her Jewish roots is equally an activist journey to archive a way of life and living that is fast fading from public memory. "Remembering," writes Susan Sontag in *Regarding the Pain of Others*, "is an ethical act, has ethical value in and of itself." Remembering is also, I would add, a political act, for in the field of memory, the politics of inclusion and exclusion has significantly framed power-dominated constructions of the mainstream and the margins. To keep personal memory alive and to pass it on to the world through poetry will always be political – the courageous and deeply humane act of voicing what is innately precarious, what can easily be lost.

An Extraordinary Ethics of the Ordinary: *Witnesses of Remembrance*

To read a poet like Kunwar Narain is to affirm witness to a new epistemological birth. Having been drawn into the quiet, unambiguous, and staunchly empathetic universe of his poetry, there is no turning back. One is led, as if by hand, from one reflection to another, from one musing to another, from one poem to another, so that page by page, there is a gentle revelation of a potent and intense alternative existential vision, and by the book's end, one has been resolutely weaned away from the world to which one is forced to return.

Widely regarded as one of India's foremost intellectuals and literary artists, Kunwar Narain (1927-2017) chose to write, primarily, in Hindi. His rich literary career encompasses over seven decades of robust writing across disciplines and genres with multiple accomplishments and honours. A recipient of the Sahitya Akademi award and the Jnanpith award, Narain's staggering oeuvre includes three epic poems, eight poetry collections, translations of world poetry, short story collections, criticism, essays, diaries, conversations, and writings on world cinema and the arts. His work has been widely translated and readers, globally, have testified to his cosmopolitan literary sensibility firmly grounded in Indian and Western thought.

As a poet reborn in the English language through exemplary translation of his work by his son, Apurva Narain, Kunwar Narain's ninety-seven selected poems in *Witnesses of Remembrance* (Westland Publications, 2021) bring forth to the English reader his unique poetic voice in all its political, philosophical and aesthetic inflections. What strikes the reader from the very beginning and with particular force, is Narain's intrinsic faith in the grace and power of verse. To write poetry well and to dwell in it are two different approaches to life and creativity. By endorsing the latter, Narain lays the framework for a new aesthetics, politics and ethics of poetry. His lived life, as Apurva Narain points out at many places in his insightful Introduction to the book, was inseparable from his poetry – "a way of life, a way to the inner sanctum of wonder and peace that literature and the arts were meant to cultivate." As an individual, he relished reclusion and in his literary career of seven decades "never launched his books, went to less than a dozen festivals, and remained reluctant about events, committees and positions of power". One understands, on reading his poems, why such reclusiveness was vital to nourish and protect that alternative view of life that imbues Narain's poetry with a rare visionary grace.

"I remember a river flowing inside my father and never growing old; a whole forest of intimate, detached trees, birds, people, stones and reveries evolving all around it; and the dark cosmic sea of a world hardly yet begun, in which we immersed," writes Apurva Narain. Kunwar Narain's poetry draws sustenance from this river of faith and begets a cosmos teeming with promises that no reality, however harsh, can break. It would not have been possible to gestate this extraordinary cosmos in conjunction and confrontation with the everyday world. A certain amount of distance would be prerequisite to its conception, creation and sustenance. This, however, is not to say that the poet's art was disengaged from life. Much to the contrary, Narain's art speaks for a brave and relentless engagement with life's poignancies, its paradoxes, its injustices and impossibilities. But this engagement is, as is characteristic of his art, though sinewy, quiet, and though profound, entirely without fanfare. Thoroughly occupied with the existential and creative exigencies of his particular poetic universe, Narain has no space or inclination for creeds, ideologies or one-stop solutions to the world's irreconcilable differences. As a poet, his self-chosen task is not to criticize or reject the world that he sees around him but to affirm its potential for generosity, growth, sanctity and love. "In a lifetime with him," states Apurva, "I never once saw him get angry, talk ill of anyone, or even swat a fly. Instead, he turned to the cosmos within, marvelling at the paradox of god in a godless world, the numen of nature in us, and the moral as an evolutionary counterpoise to the physical." This active nurturance, in thought and action, of an "other-worldliness" as Apurva calls it, remains central to Narain's vision as an artist and his intrinsic faith in the possibility of poetry to touch and transform consciousness.

In 'Hesitation', the poet carries "today's newspaper in one hand/ and poems in the other", unsure which one to read first to little children of the future, waiting "with bated breath/ to see what our epoch/ brings for them after all..." Here, the very juxtaposition of newspaper with poetry amply indicates Narain's stance. His interest and commitment, as is clear, is not so much to the outer public world as to the inner private one for he knows that it is the latter that shapes the former and not vice-versa. In 'Those Who Do Not Know', Gandhi's Ahimsa is resurrected with the words, "A path, which can always be walked/ And freedom found/ From any injustice, any oppressive/ Condition of the world." In 'God is Our Witness', the poet conjures the strange paradox of, first, affirming our biological ties to kith and kin and then negating them in the battle-field to act in accordance with *dharma*. Evoking the mythical context of the Kurukshetra, the poem is a poignant interrogation of the meaning and construction of God in the world.

In his historical poems in the collection, it is interesting to note Kunwar Narain's imagination empathetically drawn to descents, to ruins, to denouements. It is not glory that attracts him in the past, every glory being, ultimately, short-lived. What remains significant to him on the pages of time is the reconciliation with loss, failure, betrayal and defeat. In 'The Last Days of Chandragupta Maurya', he asks the king to seek "a small abode/ deep within which you will slowly go on/ getting detached from this world". 'The Estrangement of Bhartrihari' visualizes detachment as a superior form of attachment to the world without doubt or self-interest – "creating an eternal space - / not torn by people and things/ or trifling news from kith and kin", to visualize the world as "a sculptor sees a statue in stone,/ a poet sees a soul in a statue,/ a saint sees the universe in a soul…" 'Bazaar Anarkali', recalls the tragic story of love punished by history, "a savagery/ tyrannical by tradition", and sees the ghost of "a heavy-hearted prince" placing "a lighted lamp/ in the alcove of a nondescript wall". This historical memory is so painful that "beyond the endurance of so many nightfalls/ the eyes of a sky well up/ and spill out stars…"

A remarkable number of poems in *Witnesses of Remembrance* speak from an earth-centered perspective, illuminating the eco-spiritual strain that runs strongly in the poetry of Kunwar Narain. In 'The Estrangement of Bhartrihari', the poet says "neither the universe has a limit/ nor sentience…" Sentience, for Narain, is a keyword. His own sentience is awake to all entities of experience - animate and inanimate - and his intense consciousness visualizes a soul in all he sees. In fact, this extension of human sentience to acknowledge and empathize with all that the universe holds, is integral to Narain's vision and project as a poet. In 'The Beings of Stones', the poet regards the sculptor as violating the stone's integrity and finds his hands "blood-sodden". In 'The Door', the door becomes a sad reminder of "the seeds of a tree/ the legend of a grand forest/ one tied up in servitude today". In 'Next to a Paved Road', a paved road is visualized as coming up and saying – "grandpa,/ look, we have come/ so close, to live by your side now!"

In Narain's original poems, the Hindi language allows for considerable ambiguity in terms of pronouns. 'Vah' in Hindi could be 'that', 'he' or 'she' depending upon the context. The fertility of such ambiguity is considerably arrested in English where pronouns are, by nature, more revelatory of the identity of the noun. Despite this limitation, one is convinced of the fact that Narain's poetic cosmos teems with presences. In his world, nothing is subordinate, subsidiary or non-essential. His ethics repudiates the very idea of marginality. By such poetic logic, the great also has no place in Narain's oeuvre. In 'Mega Truth', for instance, he expresses anguish on account of "the endangered lives of our/ tiny child-sized truths", anxious that the mega truth will be "a giant machine, an assembly/ of countless circling cogs." 'Living an Ordinary Life', again, asserts the value of the commonplace over the exceptional by pointing out how living the commonplace life in all its sanctity, is an exception too – "Living ordinary lives too/ people have been seen/ quietly getting martyred".

This extension of sentience to every single object and experience leads the poet to contemplate an existential minimalism. Note, for instance, the Beckettian poem 'Buried in the Earth Up to the Neck'. Here, the body of the protagonist being buried up to the neck, it is only the face that enters into communion with the world. And yet, Narain insists that this face with its five organs of sense, is more than enough, to participate in life's drama and to leave it enriched – "a billion times bigger/ than the world could be/ a humanesque idea". The world represents, as he points out in 'The Killing of the Heron', "the bad times/ of a man with an axe/ hatcheting his own roots..." This tide of violence and self-destruction can be turned only through the vital force of love. "Laughter is also a kind of nearness," the poet asserts in 'Nearness' and in each poem emerges the necessity of establishing communion with the world in order to embrace and heal its paradoxes. In Narain's existential minimalism, one does not need much to live a peaceful life. "...somewhere inside of us, a corner/ where the schism between earth and sky/ between people and God/ is the least..." is enough.

One marvels at the committed task of translation that has brought these precious poems into being. Translation can be an arduous project given the quiet elegance of Narain's verse and the absence of precedence of such commonplace yet profound and dignified simplicity in the English language. The endeavour can be further challenging when the relationship between the poet and the translator is as intimate as the father-son bond is. While proximity does have its advantages, intimacy often leads to an erosion of objectivity – a vital consideration for a translator, however subjective the act of translation may be. It goes to Apurva Narain's immense credit as a translator to not have lost the requisite critical distance in bringing to birth his father's poems in English. Further, he uses his intimate knowledge of his father's mind and life to considerable advantage in resolving the ambiguities of translating between languages, his subjective choices in translation speaking for the original poems with felicity and substantial poetic authority.

Poetry, for Kunwar Narain, "is not a declaration, but a witness" and "even if one wants one cannot stop/ its testimony in language". "There are some words/ that if abased/ leave life and language/ of their own accord," writes the poet in 'Words that Disappear'. His entire life was an active crusade to preserve the words and sentiments that mattered. For these poems to not have found a life in English, would have been a grave injustice to the English language. The repertoire of Indian Writing in English stands richer and prouder by these graceful translations. Prouder, however, stands our nation in offering to the world the witnesses of remembrance of a rare poet who spent a lifetime interpreting indefatigably and with unsparing vigilance, the meaning of existing as an ordinary, finite being in an infinite world.

On Writing like a Woman: Paul Kaur's *The Wild Weed*

In her very perceptive Introduction to Paul Kaur's verse, Nirupama Dutt makes, among other significant observations, a point that I cannot help returning to, again and again. Dutt writes, "The power of Paul's poetry in her journey from the personal to the overtly political, as in the past few years, is that she has never tried to write like a man. It is a woman's vision and the objects that surround her that makes her able to express herself with a rare ease and make a worthy point." Dutt's statements are borne out by every single poem in this thoroughly pathbreaking collection that offers a unique perspective into female identity, accomplishment, emotion, resolve, honesty, philosophical acuity and sheer power. These sixty-five poems in *The Wild Weed* (Red River, 2021) have been edited and translated from the original Punjabi by Arvinder Kaur with such skill, emotive intimacy and poetic empathy that reincarnating into the form of the target language, they hardly read like translations. There is no fuzziness, no uncertainty, no brittleness or lack of lustre. No sooner has one been touched by the book's gracefulness than the knowledge of these verses as having been reborn in another language is conveniently and completely forgotten. The reader swims through the collection with complete confidence and fulfilment, grateful that no meaning has been lost.

In her poem 'Love', Paul Kaur transcends narrow notions of amorous love to envisage it as a profound emotion directed to the self as also to the world that it permeates and inhabits. And yet, the poet's love is not of the airy spiritual kind that has no transaction with the materiality of the body. Her distinctive brand of love responds robustly and sensitively to both the senses and the spirit and stands powerfully poised, embracing both:

>...I am a born lover
>filled with love to the brim
>a glance, a touch, a moment
>is just an alibi
>to delve deep within
>where I flow like a stream
>or sometimes like a river
>where I wander like a cloud
>or be the ocean.
>Yes, the ocean.

On the face of authentic and overwhelming writing like this, one is tempted to interrogate what it means to write like a woman. Is writing by women primarily sentimental and emotive? Does writing like a woman always involve radical, subversive and feminist writing? Is professing to write like a woman an essentialization of womanhood? The questions are many but the answer, to speak honestly, would be broadly one, i.e. to write like a woman is to consciously summon one's gendered sense of being a woman to one's thinking and writing in the world in the exact way that one summons one's national, linguistic, historical, sexual or cultural identity to one's writing. This gender identity-consciousness is not exclusive and is likely to coexist with other identity-consciousnesses but it will always be there.

T.S. Eliot, commenting on the admirable poetry of Marianne Moore in the 1930s, concluded his essay on her with one 'final and magnificent compliment', namely, "one never forgets that it is written by a woman...but one never thinks of this particularly as anything but a positive virtue." In an infamous interview at the Royal Geographic Society in 2011, V.S. Naipaul said, in denigration of women writers, that, "I read a piece of writing and within a paragraph or two I know whether it is by a woman or not." For a woman who chooses to write like a woman, this, I would say, is the highest praise and in Paul Kaur's poetry, it comes across in its staggering diversity and plenitude of theme, language and image.

Her metaphors, one notes, are disarmingly simple and bafflingly profound. In 'Relationships', she compares relationships to new clothes ('a new suit') whose magic lasts only as long as they are not worn. In 'On Wearing Sandals', sandals become a metaphor for habit, for a way of life that though not always desirable or convenient, is comfortable. In 'Bonsai', bonsai establishes itself as a metaphor for a diminished modernist way of life against the magnanimity of an old agrarian lifestyle. In 'Within My Self', rage and agony are described as "weaponry" for an insecure self, to be abandoned on the route to maturity. An open door becomes a metaphor for acceptance of life in the poem 'Life'. In 'Don't Envision a Home', home is symbolic of both warmth and bondage.

The subject of Paul Kaur's poetry is the poet herself or rather, the poetic self that sees the world as an extension of its own inner being. The entire collection, one observes, is an intense and sustained philosophical conversation with the self. Here are multiple voices – curious, humorous, pensive, nostalgic, rapturous, despondent and satiric – but the dominant tone of the collection is that of the reflective, the meditative and the reassuringly tranquil. Several poems here are passionately political in their spirited questioning of a consistent State politics of discrimination and othering but the poet's faith in love and humanity remains invincible. "...we now/ refuse to be measured/ and weighed" she writes in 'Proofs'. In 'The Life of a Question Mark', she insists that "The no man's land/ is not to consolidate/ your position of assault/ but a place to untie the knots,/ to undo the burdens." In 'This Country is Mine Too', she evocatively conjures the shared linguistic, literary, cultural and emotional heritage of India and Pakistan.

"... Paul is Every Woman," writes Arvinder Kaur in her Translator's Note and in this statement, as readers of *The Wild Weed* will discover, there is no exaggeration. Like a wild weed her determination takes birth incessantly, searching, as Sukrita Paul Kumar points out, "for her own original". Paul Kaur's literary accomplishments in Punjabi are well-known. One looks forward, through this aesthetically designed book by *Red River*, to her memorable introduction to the English-speaking world.

Poised between Contraries: Ram Krishna Singh's *Silence: White Distrust*

Can mental spaces engage in a chromatic dialogue? Can colours be narrativized? Can contrary impulses generate a meaningful conversation? Is it possible to find a poetic rhythm for the darkening world that has been ours ever since the Covid'19 pandemic set in? As crisis follows crisis in these difficult times and existent words recurrently fall short of expressing new, unimagined realities, one wishes one had something more concrete than language to work with and cast one's feelings immortally to memory. "Language in art," says Harold Pinter, "remains a highly ambiguous transaction, a quicksand, a trampoline, a frozen pool which may give way under you, the author, at any time. But as I have said, the search for the truth can never stop. It cannot be adjourned, it cannot be postponed. It has to be faced, right there, on the spot." For poet-academic-critic R.K. Singh too, truth-seeking is a responsibility that cannot be shrugged off by the committed artist, no matter how difficult the trials faced. In *Silence: White Distrust*, the poet attempts the daunting creative challenge of forging a new poetic rhythm to express the new pandemic experience of disillusionment, fractured chronological time, acute biological consciousness and an alienating isolation from the social world. What is remarkable is that the attempt, besides meeting unquestionable success, reaches into the depths of philosophical questioning to offer new perspectives on life and the potential of the human mind to map its paradoxes.

In his Introduction to *Silence: White Distrust* (Editorial Ave Viajera S.A.S., 2021), the poet writes:

Covid-19 lockdown has been a physically, mentally and emotionally challenging experience. Living in isolation in constant fear, suffering strict social and personal distancing, there has been a gradual rise of 'distrust' in all that was positive, self-regulating, and internally strengthening or uplifting. My silent reflections within, and observations without, exposed to me my personal, as well as socially larger, loss of hope and faith that embed spirituality. I noticed the trend in my recent poetic expression and discovered that it was possible to develop a new collection of poems with a thread of silence and distrust running through it. It also seemed possible to do a long experimental haiku-tanka-haiku linked verse....

The entire collection is composed in the fabric of a linked haiku-tanka-haiku sequence that not only appears to replicate the experience of pandemic slow time but conjures in sincere, heartfelt rhythms the despondency and sanitized silence of our days. Singh's poetry, as one reads through it, records the minutiae of our everyday lives with infallible accuracy and stark realism. Strewn across it are familiar landmarks of desire, unfulfillment, waiting, conjecture, failure, disappointment and loss. Singh's evocative imagination finds powerful metaphors for emotional states in the most mundane objects of our daily world – "empty chairs", "stain-dried lingerie", "spiders' network/ between two photo frames", "broken bangles", and "the city's garbage". The observations are neither extraordinary in themselves nor worth pondering over out of context. But through their rare felicity of association in Singh's poetry, they derive a potency that transforms them into three-dimensional architectural images of memorable strength and beauty.

Throwing light on the significance of his title, Singh writes, "Silence is positive; White too has positive connotations, but Distrust is negative. White Distrust is ironical; it is a harmless fib. There is no moralising, lecturing, or teaching." The idea, one realizes, is to sketch experience sharply poised between contraries. On the one hand is the overwhelming regime of silence with its epistemological, creative and poetic possibilities. On the other, however, is the constant and poignant sense of distrust that inhibits the mind from settling down comfortably into this space of silence. Here is a vivid and vibrant interaction of two opposing modes of feeling – silence with its connotations of fertility, expansiveness, absorption, acquiescence and peace, and distrust with its echoes of interruption, destructive questioning, faithlessness and disjunction. The accomplishment of the book rests on the delicate but firm balance established between these powerful opposing emotional forces. It is to Singh's immense credit as a poet that he never disregards the unspectacular truth to conquer the glamorous falsehood and allows them both to stand as they are, sans regret and sans illusion. In *Silence: White Distrust,* there is no obliteration of one category of experience by the other but rather, a unique expression of their cohabitation. If silence is spatial, distrust is projected as temporal so that the two remain ceaselessly poised in a perpendicular relationship, commenting and reflecting on each other through these monologic verses of confident elegance.

Silence, yes, but why distrust, one might be prompted to ask? Also, one wonders if these are entirely topical poems that derive their shape and sensibility from the context of the difficult pandemic? A close reading of the collection amply illustrates that the answers to both questions are linked. The distrust is dominant only because though appearing during the pandemic, these are not exclusively or merely pandemic poems. Born out of long drawn-out years of Singh's constant poetic searching for permanent existential truths, these poems claim for their creative site, the ageing human body and a mind wizening towards omniscience. For Singh, the body through its needs, demands, rituals, illusions and fallibility, establishes itself as the most significant medium of experience. The fact of ageing and distrust of the body marks itself indelibly in these poems:

> things get hairy, scary
> with body failure
> ailments pop up
> spirit dries up
> mind disconnects
> hesitating
> to take the first step through–
> stands at the door
> unhappy
> with how I look and
> feel right now
> seek a best version
> and just look within

It is worth noting how the spatial breaks in the poem underline the sense of disconnection, hesitation, faltering and repair. The rhythm is that of the colloquial, speaking voice and yet, the arrangement of the lines graphically on the page compounds its meanings manifold. "The white space between any two haiku and tanka adds to the sense of silence or peace," explains Singh. "It adds to the sense of Meditation too. The verses become meditative as Silence is poetically and spiritually meditative, but its rhythm is disturbed by the rising feeling of Distrust." Consider the following set:

> earthy body
> nights of silence
> fear in mirror
> return to the river
> echoing hollowed sound
> long waiting
> short consultation–
> ophthalmologist
> morning smog–
> an asthmatic with grandson
> coughing restlessly
> on the terrace even
> a limping crow seeks fresh air

The fragility of the body is paramount here and yet, one realizes that this fragility is not only physical or individual. It is, in the larger sense, a condition and imperative of life itself, of the earth, of human myopia, and the thread of existence that inevitably runs from one generation to another. Even the mirror and the crow then, become a part of this uncertainty and distrust, reflecting it and responding to it. Consider again, the following set of poems:

> pre-monsoon ramble
> wilderness in harmony–
> worlds within world
> hail stones
> lashing mango florets
> my car too:
> I fear thunder squall and rain
> leaking roof and wetting bed
> wild sugar cane
> no animals savor
> ageing monsoon

Here again, the poet leaves us amazed by the symbolic registration of the progress of time through telling images – pre-monsoon rambles, lashing mango florets and the ageing monsoon. The temporal pace of these poems merits observation as the reader is constantly made aware of the steady flow of moments and seasons in a cyclical frame. Singh's economy, terseness, sharpness and precision of expression deserve special attention as does his mastery over poetic form. The haiku and the tanka are highly challenging poetic forms by reason of their sheer minimalism, their syllabic discipline and their ability to speak more only through less. Independent, self-referential and self-explanatory units of meaning and thought, the haiku and tanka demand a deep acquaintance with techniques of condensation, reflection, refraction and amplification. The haiku-tanka-haiku sequence that Singh crafts in the book bespeaks volumes for his expertise and experimentation in minimalism, transforming the linked sequence into an evocative narrative of colour and a dense chromatic dialogue between the myriad hues of the mind. Each haiku and tanka has its own distinct subjectivity here as it formulates its personal perspective of the world. And yet, there is a strong etiological force spurring the reader on from one poem to another so that in its totality, the sequence acquires a grand epical quality and becomes a poignant litany for our times.

Tranquil yet restless, linear yet cyclical, multi-layered yet unified, fragmented yet compound, R.K. Singh's *Silence: White Distrust* that includes a Spanish translation by Joseph Berolo, Bogota, Colombia, is a singular success in the poetic ambition of translating emotional colour into language and engaging contrary ideas in an insightful colloquy. Travelling through the piece which is now included in the poet's latest collection *Against the Waves: Selected Poems* (New Delhi: Authorspress, 2021), is a journey through life's outwardness into the deep, inward recesses of the self. As a reader and critic, one realizes that an encounter with this book shall remain memorable and worthy and that these poems shall continue to be valued both for their independent lustre and for the astounding brilliance that they impart to the unfathomable wisdom of life.

An Assertion of Sisterhood: Sanjukta Dasgupta's *Unbound: New and Selected Poems (1996-2021)*

> "*Male authors of the world's patriarchal epics blame*
> *The bewitching femme fatales who seem bereft of shame*
> *But the heroes insist they need such beauties as their brides*
> *In the killing fields and theatres of war, like trophies by their sides.*"
> — 'Sita and the Golden Deer'

One can hardly be convinced of the wealth, fluency, and dexterity of sarcasm until one arrives at the poetry of Sanjukta Dasgupta. Linear, measured, suave and highly dissident, Dasgupta's poems stand out by their remarkable ability to compress social criticism in bold and geometrically precise sarcastic strokes. Keki Daruwalla calls her poems "trigger-tense poetry at its best" and one would be hard put to challenge the observation.

Unbound: New and Selected Poems (Authorspress, 2021) is Dasgupta's seventh book of poems that along with her new pieces, brings together the best of her work from her six former collections. There is a wide range of subjects here – poetry, pandemic, memory, history, love, loss, negotiation, social injustice, nature's bounty and more.

What, however, strikes the reader with particular force in most of these poems is their consistent articulation of the woman question – women's socio-cultural status, identity, historical and ideological stereotyping, ways of rebellion, and possibilities of emancipation.

In Dasgupta's poetry, there is no obliqueness or ambiguity, no dilly-dallying with metaphor, no laboured linguistic games. As feminist scholar and critic, her terrain is clearly political and her focus, pre-eminently, on her ideas. Her feminism too, one realizes, has a wide intersectional base. From mythological and fictional women across ages and cultures to everyday women of all ages and classes in homes, kitchens, workplaces and dreams – Dasgupta converses with all. In 'To Avantisundari', she speaks to the 9th century Prakrit poet, wife of scholar-dramatist Rajshekhar – "Your footsteps unseen/ Provoke, tantalize./ Till a sister ten centuries young/ Continues what you, incomparable Avantisundari,/ Began" - establishing a communion between her and the vernacular women writers of the nineteenth century in India. 'In Memoriam' is a tribute to the socialite Naina Sahni who was murdered in 1995 and her dead body burnt in a tandoori oven – "Did you not see your tragedy on their brows?/ Powerless Circe, futile Urvasi,/ Did you take it too easy, alas?"

In 'Mrinal's First Letter', the poet focuses on Mrinal, the protagonist of Tagore's famed feminist short story 'Streer Patra' ('The Wife's Letter') – "Mrinal like her elder sister Nora/ In a faraway world/ Shut herself out from the hypnotic/ Humiliating, terrifying sacred space". Sita, Kali, Durga, Manasha, Meera, Saraswati, Chandalika, Chitrangada, Circe, Medusa, Radha, Helen, Draupadi, Eve – all wander freely across Dasgupta's poetic canvas in a tight, empathetic bond of sisterhood, voicing and reinforcing each other's stories as they open their arms to embrace women globally.

However, the figure that watermarks Dasgupta's feminist oeuvre with the greatest potency is Lakshmi. Lakshmi or *Lokkhi* in Bengal is not merely the goddess of wealth and good luck but also a powerful cultural trope of the patriarchal stereotyping of women. The Bengali word '*lokkhi*' has several connotations – good, tranquil, pure, auspicious, benevolent. While as an adjective, it can be and is often applied irrespective of gender, for centuries, its use has been typically reserved for women.

The ideal girl/woman scripted by patriarchy is the '*lokkhi meye*' – shy, quiet, docile, dutiful and sacrificing. Dasgupta rightly compares this construct of the '*lokkhi meye*' or Lakshmi to the Victorian idea of the 'Angel in the House'. Implicated in the idea of '*lokkhi*' are also, as Dasgupta clearly points out, biases of caste and class as only high-born women of the upper class could aspire to this ideal. Thus, in the poem 'Gora's Re-birth' based on Tagore's novel *Gora*, Gora's realization that the maid "Lachhmia and the rarefied Lakshmi/ Are indissolubly entwined" remains, in its egalitarian spirit, revolutionary even today.

Dasgupta's 'Lakshmi' is critical of her status from the very beginning. In 'Lakshmi', she is deafened by prayers – "*Give us more, more, more/ More than another/ Give me more, mother/ More than everyone else*". "The anthem," she realizes, "is the same everywhere" and regrets having to, immortally, listen to it. In 'Lakshmi Unbound: A Soliloquy', Dasgupta's Lakshmi resents her enforced docility and domesticity:

I just can't be Lakshmi
I have to break the silence

My wealth is not jewels
My wealth is my gypsy spirit

Rebelling against patriarchal imposition, Lakshmi seizes her feminist binary – "I don't want to be Lakshmi/ I am Alakshmi/ Trap me if you can!" Alakshmi or *Olokkhi* in Bengali is *Lokkhi*'s binary opposite – loud, unruly, wilful, inauspicious. Alakshmi is Lakshmi unbound from her fetters of enforced domesticity, patriarchal expectation and self-abnegation. She is Dasgupta's defiant feminist who refuses to be scripted, hedged and spoken for by patriarchy, capitalism or consumerism. Asserting her control over her body, mind and tongue, Alakshmi advocates a strong earth-centric ethic as she walks free into possibility and promise.

In 'Sita Meets Lakshmi', Dasgupta attempts a radical feminist reading of the Ramayana with the golden deer symbolized as Alakshmi or Lakshmi Unbound. Drawn to the deer, Sita steps out of the *lakshmanrekha* to claim her freedom – "Sita felt Lakshmi's firm clasp/ As her chains clattered to the ground!" Given that Sita is widely believed to be the incarnation of Goddess Lakshmi, her association with Lakshmi Unbound is also an attempt to reclaim her authentic identity as a free woman.

To focus on Dasgupta's strong feminist leanings is not to deny the wide thematic and emotional range of *Unbound*. The 135 poems in this powerful collection constitute a bold social commentary on the hypocrisy, fanaticism and decadent morality of our times with a firm faith in the redemptive power of poetry. However, what lingers in our minds long after it has been read, is its staunch avowal of an empowered pan-cultural sisterhood.

Rebirth of Perception: Shekhar Banerjee's *The Fern-Gatherers' Association*

From a collection of poems curiously titled *The Fern-Gatherers' Association* (Red River, 2021), the reader's expectations are indeterminate. How do pteridophytes, one muses, feature in these poems? Does the book embody a specialized biologist's gaze or are these reflections of the more universal nature-lover who is irresistibly drawn towards the profusion, spontaneity and density of ferns as a counteragent to life's incremental malaise?

Winding one's way through the seventy-one poems that this book encloses, the reader realizes that in the company of words manoeuvred with deft artistry and an intricate poetic design, the experience of reading will, always and by far, exceed expectations. Resolutely but noncommittally, *The Fern-Gatherers' Association* invites entry and participation into a way of being, belonging and arranging the self around a world that is animated with sentience, emotion and vision.

Contrary to what the title seems to promise, pteridophytes or pteridomaniacs remain far from these poems. Textured in and through them, rather, is the multifarious and multi-layered life that we live everyday with its divergent patterns of longing, love, loss, sickness, nostalgia, memory, displacement and death. And yet ferns, at a denser metaphorical level, offer an organic understanding of the book's spirit, philosophy and vision.

To me, the pinnately compound worldview that this collection offers is, intensely, fern-like. Central to Shekhar Banerjee's poetics is an ontological borderlessness. His is a world with no hierarchies between the living and the non-living, let alone between species or humans. Characteristic of these poems and of Banerjee's distinctive perception as a poet is his deep comprehension of the entanglements of life's animate and inanimate spheres and his use of a diction of sentience to establish patterns of signification and relationships. In 'My Private Tutor's Crows', the sky is "the eye/of the galaxy" and the universe is "one-eyed". In 'Homeless', the slippers are somnambulists who walk to the playground where "an elderly and freckled sky sleeps with the stars,/ planets and the core of the galaxy/ like a homeless family". In 'Sign Language', the poet writes:

> A path is a child of a road; it understands the need
> to follow the family
> It ambles in a forest in spring
> to come back to a highway's arms before
> the autumn sets in

True to his compound experience of the organic unity of the world's materiality, Banerjee's poems become the warp and weft of a rare fabric of ontological co-determination. As inhabitants of the world, our sense of being is determined by the other beings – animate and inanimate - that surround us. In 'Running Up the Cliff', "the neighbouring mountains" must be consulted before a decision concerning the self is made. In 'The Liles and a Hoe', the mountains are busy "feeding a night to a hen/ so that it can crow in the morning, full of noise/ of the lilies and a hoe". 'The Calcutta Shop', again, weaves the sights and sounds of both energy and entropy, glory and bereavement, antiquity and modernity of the city of Calcutta into a poem of great tenderness and empathy:

> I juxtapose my relatives with each tree that has fallen
> defending a house, an idea, a city or a settlement
> as ordinary soldiers always do
> and I watch the lanes and bylanes of Calcutta issue
> obituaries for an undivided family
> for every dead tree – I write an epitaph:
> 'Here lived Arjun Das (43 years), Palash Das (11 years)
> and Dolonchampa Das (38)
> They are survived by us'

Nourished by an anthropomorphic vision, Banerjee's images astound by their heightened awareness of life's depth, variety and innate paradoxes. In 'The Calcutta Shop', the Howrah Bridge is "the feeding breast of this city". Letters in 'Letter Sorting House' are "unopened sleep at night". In the poem 'Cemeteries of Lettuce, Lamb and Fish', the refrigerator is both womb and cemetery and a constant guardian to "dead stories". In 'X', the poet urges a comparison of the self with a leap year "a shortage,/ without reaching out to any conclusion/ about those things/ which we generally term 'X'. 'In a Zoo' finds the sea a blind, "prehistoric animal" that is "fastened to the sky/ and vastness is its bondage".

Anxiety over the Pandemic and its new normal loom large over these poems. In 'Property of the Eye', Banerjee observes:

This is a time of knowing too much
of either love or death
and drawing a chalk line around yourself;
now you are a continent

In 'Loss', the poet attempts to explore "the tendencies/ of being alone" beyond the necessity of "sanitation". In 'Sickness', the poet declares – "I have a hospital in my breath" and takes care to wash and dry his masks "as if,/ they are my dead faces for the week". But above all, what distinctly renders this collection a firm testimony to the existential upheavals and philosophical crisis of the Pandemic is its serried reflections on the idea of home, the enclosed domestic space, the uses of solitude and the anthropometry of sleep. Being forced by the new normal to turn things inside out, Banerjee stations his subjectivity on the other side of the telescope to look at things minimally and within the wider web of their connected ambience.

In many ways, therefore, to read *The Fern-Gatherers' Association* is to opt for a retreat into a different mode of consciousness and living where the self is an additive of all the 'others' that surround it. Walking through the landscape of these poems is an exercise in mindfulness and compassionate attention whereby each 'other' is identified intimately as a kin of the self - the fern-gatherer whose identity is, like the fern lovingly gathered, always compound, composite and plural. Deep in their philosophy, penetrating in their intellect, addictive in the languorous sonority of their diction and vigorous in their faith, these poems will be staunchly embraced each time the self is curious to know the world it lives by.

A Romance with Life: Smita Agarwal's *Speak, Woman!*

A collection of poems by a woman poet and entitled *Speak, Woman!* (Red River, 2021) is likely to invite certain speculations, especially if the poet's reputation as a feminist precedes the book. Urging women to break the walls of silence, fostering a female community by inspiring conversation and exchange of experiences, and shaping assertive, speaking women through consciousness-raising sessions, have been significant agendas within the feminist movement. It is pardonable, therefore, to assume that Smita Agarwal's book is animated by a kindred spirit, that it is likely to be a rant, a wake-up call, a weighted exclamation of unrest and of rage. One is surprised, therefore, to be acquainted with its breezy, carefree, self-governed spirit, its noncommittal turns of thought, its amusing postures and its disarmingly candid diction. Instead of the categorical feminist fare that one has been expecting it to bare, here is a kaleidoscopic celebration of life, a full-fledged embracing of its myriad shades, and an assertion of a selfhood that is gaily ageing, fallible and female.

This is not to say that Agarwal has given respite to her sharpness or abandoned her trade. A substantial number of poems in this collection are flamboyantly subversive.

Note, for instance, 'Parrot', a mother's advice to her newly-married daughter that echoes the tone of early Prakrit feminist poetry. Here, the man (husband) is described as a parrot "flitting from tree to tree, / pecking at, nibbling ripe/ fruit, leaving them/ mostly ruined." The woman's (wife's) task is to "put it in a gilded cage" and to "teach it: to call out your name./ Your name, only your name,/ over and over again." Observe how the idea of inhibition, confinement and conditioning is gloriously subverted here so that instead of leading to the woman's imprisonment, marriage heralds, in this poem, the beginning of male incarceration. In 'Giving it Back', another poem set on the conjugal theme, the wife consistently learns from the husband the art to break the heart "like an eggshell or a bone" and masters "the grin of pain" only to use these tactics in later life to wreak her revenge upon him. Her Instagram post now mints "a million likes" while the husband has his face "ground in grime". 'To a Daughter on Raksha Bandhan', subverts once again, the cultural tradition of men protecting women. Agarwal reminds:

> Recall, how Kunti had to
> dispossess herself
> of a son,
> Sita, walk into fire,
> despite all the wrists
> adorned with sacred thread.

"Be your own friend," she advises women for "when a tooth aches,/ labour pains lash out,/ or, a diseased body part/ rebels, you learn/ no one can protect you from pain." The sacred thread, she urges, should be wrapped by the woman on her own wrist "to help yourself/ when, god forbid, in need."

Many poems in this collection constellate around a powerful gerontological identity – the acquiescence, even celebration of the biological, emotional and philosophical process of ageing, this spending of another coin "from the more or less/ empty purse of life." In these poems are the nostalgia of youth but also the contentment at having spiritedly traversed time to arrive at this moment. In 'At Sixty-Three', the poet experiences "an odd sort of joy" that makes her want "to just stand up/ and clap!" Advancing years have their own share of honest regret – "every bearded old man/ on a bicycle is now/ that first love I long ago/ let go and lost." Ageing is also witnessing our loved one's age – "superannuation and redundancy/ are a huge canvas,/ newly bought". And yet, one desires to "usher in the new day,/ welcome the chorus of birds". 'Grandmother Diaries', 'Debut' and 'Mammarian Milonga' celebrate the joys of motherhood found anew and redoubled in grandmotherhood. In the first poem, the child's squeal awakens the grandmother's deep maternal instinct to offer it milk despite a body incapable of doing it. In the mock-epical 'Debut', the two year-old grandson becomes "a hero, of the stature of the/ adolescent Ram culling in the forest/ Subaahu and Mareecha,/ the baby Krishna, slaying Pootana" and only because of his fearlessness of house lizards. In 'Mammarian Milonga', the pun on mammarian is unmissable and unforgettable for the poet-speaker wishes to activate her mammarian glands into a milonga dance. Though immensely playful, the poem also draws attention to popular visual representations of women which are hardly authentic and are crafted, most-often, to suit the male gaze. 'The Rapist at My Door' is another brilliant poem that compares ageing to a physical and psychological violation that can only lead to the void of death:

> Strands of hair on my head
> change colour.
> The lines on my face multiply.
> Time stands still and yet, ticks on;
> my eyes bore through the thick
> panelled door
> attempting to figure out when
> this game'll be over.
> I know I will go down.
> Gun blazing is how I want to go.

Ageing is also a profound metaphor in the overtly political poems 'The Indian Parliament' and 'Self-Goal' where the nation is projected as an ancient being stirring in sleep, sometimes, in awakening. However, to me, the most poignant poem in the collection is its very first piece – 'Guru Mantra'. The word 'guru' in Sanskrit means one who dispels all darkness. The poem that describes an ambiguous encounter between a male guru and a twenty-five year-old aspiring female artist, raises complex questions regarding knowledge, gender, power and victimization.:

> I wanted to learn. To read and write this language.
> In my time and location there was no other way.
> This was the only school.
> If I left, I would remain unlettered in the art.

The aspiring artist remains - to be asked to unhook her blouse and to sing with the guru's palm on her throat – "the sparrow paralysed before the swaying hood of the Cobra." In this poem is both an affirmation of women's vulnerability and limited agency, and her sheer perseverance. The poem's conclusion – "And I've been singing, since!", however, is loaded with ambiguity. Is it the guru mantra that the woman has been singing since then or has she, indeed, arrived at her vocation as an artist?

Throughout the thirty-eight poems in this book, Smita Agarwal's tone remains self-amused, taking on, by turns, the dry and juicy intonations of her subjects. The first-person and third-person points-of-view alternate in these pieces, offering a back and forth of emotional identification and distancing so that reading the book gives one the experience of looking through an album of photographs captured from various angles. Here is, as Anisur Rahman describes in his *Afterword* to the book "a long romance" with life lived to the hilt. There have been compromises too, perhaps, as the poem 'War' articulates – "She's ... just an ordinary woman/ with a cowardly heart,/ who couldn't let loose/ The monster of War, / hurting children,/ damaging children,/ gobbling up their lives." But the poems, on the whole, breathe gratefully to life and are untouched by rancour. To conclude, again with Anisur Rahman's words, "Here is a gyre of poems in which life dances firmly on an oval floor now, now precariously on its toes."

Wo(e)manhood and the Architecture of Feminist Solidarity: Usha Akella's *I Will Not Bear You Sons*

When Usha Akella's *I Will Not Bear You Sons* was published by Spinifex Press in March, 2021, it found itself embroiled in an avalanche of controversy. Men's rights activists from across India and its diaspora took personal offence to the book's title and to random excerpts from its eponymous poem that accompanied the book's various media promotions, especially the lines:

> I will abort every male fetus I bear,
>
> I will live to ensure there are no more sons,
>
> I will live to see your bloodline cross over
>
> with you to the other side

Readers that included both men and women read these lines as invincible proof of the blatant promotion of misandry, toxic feminism and male foeticide. The book's writer and its publisher faced a storm of adverse and abusive reactions on social media and were subject to outrageous threats, both verbal and otherwise. It is owing only to their sheer grit and artistic commitment that the book endured and lives to tell its many-faceted truth.

While the reader's right to interpret a text certainly remains indisputable, what aggrieves the creative (and academic) conscience is the frequent lack of integrity summoned to the acts of reading and interpretation. Texts are both constituents and alternative (re)presentations of the world. Every text, while reflecting/refracting the world as it exists somewhere, also constitutes a universe of its own, putting forward an idiosyncratic logic of ordering its systems of relations. The task of meaning-making demands devout engagement with the entire body and spirit of a text. Interpretation has its elaborate erotics that cannot be sustained by fork-picking ideas/lines/sentiments from the text's organic body for impetuous or whimsical attention/scrutiny/consumption. In poetry, especially, where connotation and suggestion often hold sway over denotation and clear statement, the risks of misinterpretation, even for an initiated reader, run high.

Keeping the title's syntactical structure intact, one wonders if an innocuous phrase like 'I will not bake you muffins' or even an outrageous one like 'I will not bear you an orgasm' would have prompted reactions even remotely analogous to what *I Will Not Bear You Sons* met with. One suspects such phrases would have been met with the opposite reaction. What struck home in the original phrase was the (radical) affront to a clear civilizational prejudice and a deep-seated culturally-sanctioned erasure of women.

For readers well-acquainted with Indian culture, the title is symbolically loaded with an epistemology that needs no explanation. In a country where the traditional benediction showered on married women has been their ability to bear a hundred sons, the title of Akella's book frames itself as a blatant blasphemy. Today, in the backdrop of the shameful overturning of the Roe v Wade decision by the US Supreme Court, *I Will Not Bear You (Sons)* gains in foresight, hindsight, relevance and poignance, and will, perhaps, strike as blasphemous in the US too with equal vigour.

Narrativizing a planetary history of women's victimization, dispossession and suffering, and the transcultural and strategic disempowerment of women's selfhoods by patriarchal scripts of being and performance, *I Will Not Bear You Sons* is an anthem of intersectional feminist solidarity. In her poem 'Ants', Akella comes up with an interesting coinage: "woeman" which, for me, nails the collection's essential thrust. The perpetrator and the victim in this narrative remain fixed throughout the rapid shifts in geographical locales and cultural practices, as does the determination to dissent. Akella's arc is ambitious and uncompromising. From female foeticide, infanticide, arranged marriages, dowry killings and rape, to female genital mutilation, foot-binding, forced breeding of African American enslaved women, sex work, consumerism and climate change, she interrogates almost every cultural script of patriarchy. Her politics is militant, her irony unmissable, and her empathy, global.

The sixty-three poems in this book are divided into two sections, 'I' and 'We', and speak evocatively to each other, denoting a shared geography of experience, oppression and resistance. And yet, in keeping with the architecture of feminist solidarity, the two sections refuse to remain confined and interpenetrate one another with the assurance of a shared allegiance. Autobiography merges with social history and vice-versa with the result that the voice of the 'I' is validated by the 'We' and that of the 'We' is animated by the 'I'.

Pluralist and multicultural though the collection is in its feminist avowal, it is also astutely conscious of the differential power-games of culture in a globalized world. Diasporic in its anchoring, it reads cultural encounters through a postcolonial lens and attempts to resurrect the invisible and the marginal within mainstream cultural dialogues. In 'I Can't/Won't Write Like a White Male Poet', the poet's claim to "speak with a tongue 10,000 centuries long" is an attempt to place herself firmly within the rich and ancient oral traditions of the East, but also within a tradition of feminist performance symbolized through Kali's outstretched tongue ("…we stick out our tongue at countries that try to claim us," she writes in 'Poems I Can't Write').

Constant within the axis of these poems is the writer's inherited worldview: "the Brahmin Niyogi sensibility" which she relentlessly attempts to explore, excavate, critique, re-assess and sift for what is tenable, valuable and worth handing over to the next generation. In 'Simple Equations in the Niyogi Worldview', Akella brings out the hollow binaries between the traditional and the modern, the cultured and the uncultured, the East and the West. This is a strain that inheres in most of her poems about India/ns. In 'Darbar of Frogs', for instance, the binaries find metaphors in the figures of the frog and the swan, and the forced turning of the latter into the former:

"We'll pluck her feathers now to make her a frog."
They nodded unanimously.

> The astrologers looked thoughtful making many calculations in their
> notebooks. "It is time," they nodded agreeably. The priests cleared their
> throats and began to recite Sanskrit slokas. Manu, the head priest, was a
> very busy frog these days. He had hundreds of skinning-the-swan events to officiate.

The reference to Manu, the first Hindu law-giver, makes Akella's stance explicit here. But even otherwise, what she describes has heart-wrenching resonances for the Indian reader. While the loss of identity in arranged marriages (to the extent of giving the bride a new name) has been a fairly common practice in India till the last century, the country's political right-wing has, over the last few years, taken a keen interest in saffronizing/Hindu-izing the Indian identity by violently punishing difference. A spate of mob-lynchings and vigilante-attacks in the recent past, in an attempt to make the Indian populace conform to orthodox Hinduism by terrorizing difference into submission/complicity/death/erasure has dominated the Indian socio-cultural sphere, and of these, along with witch-hunts and gang-rapes, Akella's "skinning-the swan event" is a pertinent and painful reminder.

In 'Harmony', the frog's "amphibian" world is again detailed, this time with exclusive reference to the acts of cooking and eating. The rituals of preparation and serving are elaborate, the division of labour is immediately apparent and so is the culturally-sanctioned power equation between the server and the served:

> He eats....
> careful not to spill out too marked an appreciation

keeping the possibility of her pride in check, doing her a favour, multiplying her virtue.

But power, as Akella consistently notes in her poems, is a layered phenomenon and finds its own niches in which to flourish so that even this server "unseen, in the kitchen,/ sanctified by self-sacrificing labor" wields power over "a daughter-in-law who is allowed/ to chop and measure, forbidden from/ the fine act of cooking in this goddess's kitchen." 'For a Certain Kind of Woman', again, outlines how sexism in women and their uncritical participation in the patriarchal machinery of othering destroys the possibility and potential for feminist solidarity. Akella's "certain kind of woman" is neither virtue unadulterated nor the pious self-sacrificer. She is, rather, an ambitious, colluding subject of patriarchy, rigorously self-trained to fit the model of the 'angel in the house'. She raises herself to "empress of her domestic domain" by respecting every patriarchal regulation so that "her husband is a little snug ring on her finger,/ so smug, he doesn't know he is being worn.,/ thinking he wears her…". By joining hands with patriarchy, such a woman, according to Akella, "takes all of us 5½ centuries back,/ she personally immolates other women who/ are responsible for the air she breathes." "She is the kind of woman who makes a woman like me necessary," asserts the poet and rightly so, for it is only by acknowledging our shared victimhood as women and by rooting for one another that a way forward and towards the discourse of rights, justice and equality can be found.

Rejecting the overwhelming inequities of patriarchy, Akella finds nourishment in a different kind of tradition – one of brave, free and fearless women bonding in and for love. "Have I thawed at least one hard sinew in my heart?/

Am I lighter when I reach the other side?" she asks in 'Bridges' and bids us ask the same questions to ourselves every day. Solidarity can be built only on the poignant recognition of our shared vulnerability and our shared desire to conquer and be conquered by love. Akella's poetry, therefore, is keen to build bridges and connections across time, space, history, religion, culture and philosophy. Kali, Katyayini, Mary, Mirabai, Draupadi, Kamala Das, Anne Frank, Anne Boleyn, Sylvia Plath, Meena Kandasamy, Manuela Sáenz, Kamala Harris, Clara Sherman, Radha, Shakuntala, Sakhi, the unnamed African-American women who were enslaved, Turkish women immigrants, sex workers on Rosse Buurt, the Somalian girl Astur, the Delhi rape survivor Jyoti and Akella's own mother, grandmother and daughter – all hold hands across the canvas of these poems to respond to the poet's call to "harangue the stars with your voices" ('Women Speak').

There is plenty of straight speaking in these poems and yet, the craft remains immaculate. Akella is conscious not to let her politics mar her poetics and in the best of her poems is to be found a sublimation of desire, rage and hurt into the universality and timelessness of art. "For the truth is, I have not traced/ a face longingly as an embroiderer/ traces the outline of a flower," she writes in 'Not Enough'. In 'Requiode', home becomes "a newborn calf" that "often rearranges itself on its fours,/ like pieces of glass in a kaleidoscope". The intensity and exquisite tenderness of lines such as these travel like gold threadwork across the undulating fabric of this collection. Akella's language has both the quietness and force of water, her metaphors are flushed with the heat of sincere passion and her rhythm has an incantatory spirit that seems to grant her poems the strength of a prophecy.

To me, the book is the decisive dismantling of a threshold on the global map of patriarchy. "Enough! No More!" the book's cover, with its multi-hued feminine hands speaking for all women, seems to say. A palimpsest of voices offering a catalogue of injustices, these poems refuse to for/bear any longer. The eponymous poem 'I Will Not Bear You Sons' says:

> I will have daughters dead by female infanticide,
> daughters dead by dowry burning,
> daughters mutilated by ritual genital cutting,
> daughters slicing their wrists,
> daughters anemic, anorexic, stunted into size zeros.

Here is feminism at its fiercest and its most vulnerable, pouring out through a poetic conscience that recognizes its force and fallibility. There is no misandry here, no strategic planning of male foeticide, no refusal to birth or assertion to bury sons. Here is only an overwhelming pain that has no kin – the pain of annihilation of the self, of the species, of love, possibility and faith. Here is only a guttural wail for lost daughters and a creative transmutation of this pain into distilled poetry whose oracular feminist vision asserts, against the Bible and Yeats, of a second coming like

> ... the blight
> of women staking the earth,
> taking their own in every possible way ('Poems I Can't Write').

Writing Locality as Text: Abhay K's *Monsoon: A Poem of Love and Longing*

Poet-diplomat Abhay K's *Monsoon: A Poem of Love and Longing* (Sahitya Akademi, 2022) is a lyrical interweaving of two passions – his love for landscape and his ardour for tracing connections across cultures and lifeforms. The painting that features on the book's cover – 'Utka Nayika' or 'The Expectant Heroine' is drawn from the folio of Keshavadasa's well-known ritikavya *Rasikapriya* belonging to the mid-seventeenth century and encapsulates the many thematic symphonies that the book unfurls for the discerning reader.

The book cover offers to our gaze a lush, verdant grove at the centre of which is a woman looking up at the sky, her waiting exemplified by her posture and the flowers that lie scattered around her. Flora and fauna surround this 'utka nayika' on all sides, re-enacting her waiting through peacocks calling out to their mates. Desire is evocatively pictured here but so is a cosmos that, poised on harmony, is completely at home within itself. This sense of harmony, fine balance and peaceful co-existence of multifarious lifeforms is very revelatory of *Monsoon*'s essence.

A single poem of 150 quatrains, *Monsoon* describes the journey of the south-west Monsoon from the island of Madagascar across the Indian Ocean and the Indian subcontinent to the Himalayas. Its literary inspiration, quite obvious to most readers, is derived from Kalidasa's *Meghadutam* which, in Sanskrit, was the harbinger of the *sandesa kavya* or the 'messenger poem' whose plot involves two separated lovers and constitutes in the sending of a message by the one to the other. In Abhay K's *Monsoon*, however, the idea of an amorous love-letter sent to the pining beloved through the cloud-messenger is only a thinly veiled contrivance for professing a love of another kind, one that is both profoundly ecological and staunchly territorial.

The ecological thrust of Abhay K's work is not far to seek. *Monsoon* abounds in the fecundity and glory of all forms of plant and animal life – terrestrial, aquatic and aerial. There is, throughout the book, a rich sampling of the biota of the various geographical regions that the cloud traverses and lest these connections should be missed by readers, the poem is accompanied by elaborate footnotes that enhance our repertoire of geographical information in compound ways. Thus, Mantellas, we come to know, are golden or multicoloured poison frogs of the Madagascar and that the Sifaka, also known as the dancing lemur, is a critically endangered species of lemurs.

References such as these are densely embroidered in the fabric of the entire poem and are seldom, without poetic significance. The monsoon, beginning its journey from Madagascar will, for instance, see:

Traveller's palms stretching their arms in prayer
Baobabs meditating like ascetics turned upside down

Giraffe-necked red weevils necking their mates
fragrant Champa flowers – galaxies on the earth
Further ahead in Mauritius, it is awaited by:
Black River Gorges resembling an enchantress
and the seven coloured princess Chamarel
will captivate your heart, frolic with the pink pigeon
before they vanish forever from the earth

From here, it must proceed onwards "further northwest to the islands of Zanzibar,/ Red Colobus, Fischer's Turaco, Blue Duiker". The range of geographical references in *Monsoon* is stunning and encyclopaedic. Yet the urge that dominates the poem is not the catalogic or the documentary. What is, rather, at work here is a keen ecological activism that seeks to offer due space, value and representation to the intense drama of the non-human world that largely goes unseen and ignored.

Through the aerial and egalitarian vision of the monsoon, Abhay K notes the complex interpenetration of land, locality, nature, culture, community, biosphere and more. Accompanying his ecological concern in *Monsoon* is a focussed territorial concern. Every landscape, with its ecological and human wealth, is a distinct cultural script that articulates a heritage. A locality is an identifiable coordinate not only on the geographical map but on the cultural map of the globe as well. Localities are created by idiosyncratic and multilayered umbilical relationships between geography, nature and culture. As such, every locality constitutes a unique geographical and cultural fingerprint.

It is to Abhay K's astuteness as a poet and diplomat that he realizes the threat to the local in a global world and attempts to resurrect in *Monsoon* the vibrant localities of, as he puts it in his Introduction, "the Indian Ocean islands of Madagascar, *Réunion, Mauritius, Seychelles, Mayotte, Comoros, Zanzibar, Socotra, Maldives, Sri Lanka, Andaman & Nicobar and the Indian subcontinent into one poetic thread."*

Unlike the cloud-messenger in the homologous world of Kalidasa's *Meghadutam*, the contemporary cloud-messenger traversing a passage from Madagascar to Srinagar must bear witness to the mini-narratives of postcolonial and postmodern diversity that characterize this terrain and must speak for the rich localities that it encounters en route. Hence, ecological descriptions in *Monsoon* fuse with sharp territorial signifiers of landmarks, monuments, cuisines, languages, fashion, rites and rituals. Thus, Kerala's *kettuvallam* cruises, Karnataka's Tulu language, the hot springs of Rajgir, Bihar's *laai, tilkut, anarsa*, Kumbhalgarh's Badal Mahal, Chandigarh's Sukhna Lake and old Delhi's Ghalib ki Haveli at Gali Ballimaran, to mention just a handful, come together in this poem to reinstate the anthropological value and charm of locality in public memory.

Idyllic as this mode of memory-making is, it is not naive of the region's history of migration and loss. Thus, the whiffs of old Bhojpuri and Gujarati carried by the monsoon from the Indian Ocean islands will always remind the Indian speakers of these languages of a past that can, perhaps, be recovered only in the imagination. And that is why Abhay K's *Monsoon*, despite its global and public consciousness of history, ecology, and climate change, can still successfully awaken nostalgia for the small, the personal and the minor – for a mother in Chhabilapur restless for her son to return home.

Sufist Reconstruction of a Broken World: Afsar Mohammad's *Evening with a Sufi: Selected Poems*

> I'm sorry, my Lord.
> My poem is not your slave,
> it's a sickle with its head to the sky.
> My poem is not a damsel timid in your moonlight,
> it's a tiger prowling in a shadowed forest.
> My poem won't be your grand constitution,
> devoted to your happiness
> at all costs.
>
> — 'Outcast's Grief' from *Evening with a Sufi*

Not all poetry can be read with the same eye or ear. Certain poems demand to be seen and heard on their own terms, offering to the reader their own canons of understanding and appreciation in imaging an idea that, through them, has just been born into thought. Afsar Mohammad's *Evening with a Sufi* (Red River, 2022) translated from the original Telugu into English by Afsar Mohammad and Shamala Gallagher sets out to be one such thought-provoking book of poems.

A slim collection of twenty-six verses, these existentially political poems are as theoretically perspicacious as they are urgent and astounding in their overwhelming sincerity. Like Eliot's *The Waste Land*, Afsar Mohammad's *Evening with a Sufi* aesthetically documents a difficult world, especially one criss-crossed with systemic hegemony, and bereft of equality. An engagement with these poems is a direct invitation to the reader to embark on an epistemological tour into a sharp symbolic landscape that encapsulates visceral records of social meaning.

The title, to begin with, itself upholds a strong symbolism. Its 'evening' bespeaks the twilight of civilization, the personal-social moment of the unleashing of despair, and a decadent global landscape thriving on inequity and deprivation. And yet, evening, in these poems, is also the transitional period of awareness, self-reflection, evaluation, and the collective envisioning of an egalitarian dawn. These poems, therefore, become investigations and articulations of both fatigue and rest, of falling apart and re-gathering, and of old failures and new beginnings, leading us to look at the idea of the Sufi or Sufism anew.

"For me, Sufism is nothing but a tool of resistance," avers the poet, indicating how Sufism, as a philosophy, offers a vigorous counternarrative to transnational policies and practices of discrimination, marginalization, disempowerment and exclusion. "In my village Sufism, I see how people of diverse colours and castes share food, rituals and stories. As a village person, it's not a far-fetched utopia for me — but an everyday reality. My writings are nothing but reminders of that shared realm of life."

In Afsar's poems, Sufism becomes a political as well as existential search for a vision of oneness. This vision is, at the same time, philosophical and social, local and global, integrating and intimidating in the way that most revolutions are – "The drop that can swallow a desert" ('Another Word') or "Where walls are knocked down,/ we won't need the splendour of curtains" ('The Spectator is Dead') or "I always speak the language of war." ('A Green Bird and the Nest of Light')

Identity surfaces as a significant theme in this book. Most of the twenty-six poems in *Evening with a Sufi* embark on a complex exploration of identity on geographical, cultural, social, historical or linguistic terrains. However, the book's conceptualization of identity is far from monolithic. Germane to the vision of these poems is the essentially dialogic space of identity and its characterization as an ever-contingent work-in-progress.

Mark the first poem in the collection, for instance. Titled 'Name Calling', an ambiguous phrase that poignantly addresses the phenomenon of naming as an act of ab/use, the poem captures the essential seamlessness of names and identities. The protagonist of the piece is a boyhood contemporary called Usman who is visibly an/other to the speaker of the poem, the difference between them marked out distinctly in class terms and perhaps also (less evidently) in terms of physical ability – "You scared all the children/ away from the river./ A body like a wound/ peeks from your torn shirt." It is, however, to this social pariah – "the one street dog doggedly haunted by a ball" that the speaker feels affiliated in his later life:

> Now I don't see much difference between you and me.
> We are the same.[...]
> Usman, times never change
> only the roles change.

Muslim, Telugu and Third-world migrant, the poet reads the theory and experience of otherness on a number of sociological axes and through a variety of cultural lenses. In 'The Accented Word', he uses the idea of accent to explore the complex genealogies of language on the intersections of purism and cultural hegemony, contemplating variously, through the three sections of the poem, on linguistic integrity, capitalist subordination, and postcolonial erasure:

> Words
> are stillborn babies.
> Their blood has gone bad with white poison,
> their words have gone bad from the accent.
> I've been poured, shared, and bathed in white poison
> since I was little
> and now I want to speak out for myself.
> But my voice is in chains
> and my language is poisoned,
> and the language of my time is poisoned.
> We live on the brackish water of life.

While Shakespeare's Caliban in *The Tempest* felt that the colonizer's language profited him by teaching him "how to curse", Afsar's poems approach language with utmost caution, forever mindful of the possibility of trampling and obscuring buried histories of domination and betrayal. Many of the poem, here, are metapoetic in their thrust, assiduously exploring the value of meaningful postcolonial poetic creation from the inescapable inequities and ideological loopholes of language: "a market piles up words sounding like poetry" ('The Accented Word') or "How long this slavery to white poems?" ('Outcast's Grief') or again as in "Poetry: / just one dried leaf." ('Walking')

In 'A Piece of Bread, a Country, and a Shehnai', bread, music, war and pain – all come together to avow our subcontinent's shared heritage of poverty and cultural intimacy brutally shredded by politico-religious separation. In 'No Birthplace', the speaker of the poem is as much the Indian subcontinent as its hapless postcolonial citizen faced with the inability to reconcile its historical legacy of cultural plurality with the blind spots in its mythological and ideological machinery:

> Come, divide me by myself, I say.
> Not by forty-seven.
> My laughs, screams, harangues, deaths, and rapes —
> They're all yours too!

It is interesting to note how Afsar's poems consistently invigorate and socially translate the idea of spirituality through sinewy sociological imagery with the result that spirituality is transformed from a closeted and socially-indifferent personal practice to a welfare-oriented everyday social ritual. In 'Iftar Siren', the idea of fasting as self-purification is ironically brought to bear on the understanding of the hunger-stricken socially dispossessed as perpetually cleansed while the overfed victimizers walk about unconcerned:

> What a great life.
> In the holy month,
> do you see how you are all becoming pure?
> I've been like this for years
> burning in the divine fire.
> Unable to turn into ashes.
> I'm a fire-pit you try
> and try to stamp out.

Yes, the fire-pit
is tired too.

The haunting and incendiary metaphor of hunger as fire and the stomach/body as the fire-pit, tired of being stamped out or dispossessed, makes these poems powerful bandages for social injustices as well as flaming flags of protest. In 'Qibla', the posture of prayer, again, pivots on the stomach – "a belly turned deep/ into itself/ in which I obscure my body,/ feet, hands and everything/ for a long time" – suggesting the omnipotence of hunger as surpassing all acts of asocial faith. The poem concludes with considerable uncertainty of the efficacy of prayer and with an ideological pun on "arms" (arm/armament) as a means of erasing human hatred.

The stupendous yet composed energy of the book needs no forestatement. Every single word here is deftly chosen, well-placed, and tersely poised to make emotional leaps on command. The images are taut, the sentiments thoroughly grilled in the fire of creative originality, and everywhere, there is a sense of potential unruliness held firmly in check by a balanced and farsighted imagination.

In considering these poems, one must not forget, also, their complex linguistic history. Though translated from the original Telugu, the Telugu language itself includes, for the poet, "the entangled history of Urdu, Hindi and English — the languages that indeed shaped my emotional realm." Arriving into English via such multi-layered linguistic travails and travels, these exceptionally well-translated poems infuse postcolonial English with a visceral depth, a spiritual profundity and a razor-sharp urgency that would be difficult to come by in the original English.

Accompanied by a very relevant author interview and insightful essays by the translator and valuable first readers of this collection, *Evening with a Sufi* arrives, in its essential philosophy and call for humanitarian action, with a new theory and praxis for the world, determined to reconstruct rather than redeem it.

A Dialogue with Stillness: Bina's *ukiyo-e days... haiku moments*

The wonder of art acknowledges and affirms the potency of stillness, its pregnancy vouching for a revelation that is both vital and imminent. Ambitious as the thought is, is it possible to engage in a dialogue with stillness, to distil the flurry of a day into the transcendence of a moment, and to transform that moment, in turn, into a metaphoric prism for the illumination of all our hereafters? In her recent collection of poems *ukiyo-e days... haiku moments* (Red River, 2022), Bina (Sarkar Ellias) can justifiably claim to have assayed each of these tasks with remarkable felicity and quiet grace.

A form of Japanese art that flourished between the 17th and the 19th centuries, 'ukiyo-e' is a composite of three words – 'uki' (floating), 'yo' (world) and 'e' (pictures), literally meaning "pictures of the floating world". The 'floating world' referred to the theatre districts and (licensed) courtesan quarters that flourished in Japan's major cities during the Edo period and constituted an important source of attraction for the nouveau-riche of the era. Inhabited largely by courtesans and Kabuki (a traditional Japanese theatrical form) actors, this floating world, despite its low status in the social hierarchy of the times, made its impact as valuable cultural capital, its sartorial customs and mannerisms becoming quite effectively, a rage among common people.

Since paintings could be afforded only by the prosperous, the ukiyo-e artists made a distinct historical move to democratize art by being the first to experiment with woodblock prints which could be produced cheaply and in large numbers, thus making ukiyo-e widely accessible to the populace. Actors, courtesans, legends, folklore, and landscapes were some of the common subjects that marked this art, the heroic and the erotic being significant thematic notes within it.

ukiyo-e days… haiku moments revisits this memorable Japanese artform to bring to the reader a remarkable collection of 68 ukiyo-e by 28 artists from across the seventeenth to the early twentieth century, showcasing a delectable mix of the traditional and the modern in Japanese art and its unique blend of native and foreign influences. Compounding the effect of the ukiyo-e here, is a set of 62 haiku by Bina that excavate, explore and expand the meaning and value of the artworks by bringing them into dense ekphrastic conversation with her own mind and times. "My haiku travels with each of the ukiyo-e works as a companion through this journey, responding with a deep kinship I feel with the artworks," she writes in her Preface.

In this collaborative project of creativity, the haiku become a companion to the historical journey of the ukiyo-e, illuminating them in a transcultural framework which even as it asserts the omnipotent significance of art, helps draw attention to its omniscience across temporal and cultural divides. "To read a haiku," says Jane Hirshfield, "is to become its co-author, to place yourself inside its words until they reveal one of the proteus-shapes of your own life." As Bina places her contemporary and complex historical self within the sensibility of the ukiyo-e, her unravelling of meaning through the haiku becomes yet another act of seeking connection and consolation in an alienated world.

As a poetic form, the haiku establishes a constant romance with the brevity of expression on the one hand and the expanse of space on the other. Its sharp imagism helps to illumine both the moment and the emotional ambience that will render this moment organic in every context. Scale, speed, succinctness and surrealism can all work in concert within the seemingly fragile universe of the haiku to make it an emblem of and testimony to the wide-ranging historical forces within which it is birthed. The animated and tender conversation between colour, form and script in *ukiyo-e days... haiku moments* works similarly holding both word and beauty in suspension, mirroring the moment as self and self as moment, and asking us to return to the quintessential celebration of both:

> you want to be free
> but maya mesmerises-
> locks all the doors

The haiku is, often, a lesson in perception. It is characteristic of the haiku to be profoundly epiphanic and in many of her pieces, Bina ascends to that level of quiet illumination wherein an inner truth becomes simpler by the sole virtue of its lucid expression. Art, life, hope, faith, poetry, war, human vulnerability -- all emerge as important themes here. One cannot help noticing, however, the collection's loving partiality toward women. Women and their myriad-layered lives constitute a recurrent thematic motif in these poems:

into the long night
her toil of pleasure-giving
a tale of two worlds

Since in much of the ukiyo-e, the women represented were courtesans, Bina brings a profound sense of tenderness and understanding in reinterpreting their situation for modern women whose lives, in different contexts, remain emotively the same. In their intensity and in the overall poignance with which these haiku delineate women's ever-shifting roles in terms of profession, domesticity and relationships with the world, Bina evinces a deep knowledge of women's spiritual multiplicity. To Torii Kiiyonaga's delicate artwork 'Bathhouse Women', for instance, Bina, deflecting attention from the voyeuristic potential of the scene to give the bathhouse a larger cultural and political logic, responds:

a day for washing
wash away patriarchy
energise our souls

Another beautiful narrative turn in haiku is offered in response to Kitagawa Utamaro's print 'Naniwa Okita Admiring Herself in a Mirror' in which Bina imagines a different (more youthful) face emerging from the mirror. While the mirror has mostly been used as a truth-telling device in literature and a means of shattering illusion, this particular mirror becomes a gateway to the discovery of the magical self within, unmarred by the winter of time:

i see a mirage
see my youth in winter years
does the mirror lie?

With Chobunsai Eishi's 'The Courtesan Hanaogi of the Ogiya Brothel', Bina communicates thus:

> within the prose
>
> of her pleasure-house living
>
> she breathes poetry

Here is a mature and perceptive weaving of art and life -- a recognition of art as art and of life as life with the potential of building strong and tenable bridges across them. It is noteworthy how each haiku stands independently even as it adds a significant hermeneutic or experiential dimension to the ukiyo-e, imparting a certain luminosity to this book. There is a distinct sensation of time-travel in this collection, of moving through the slow whirl of centuries while remaining undivorced from the crises and flavours of the present:

> realisation
>
> we were not born violent
>
> let's repair ourselves

Empathy becomes a powerful voice in *ukiyo-e days* as Bina's haiku touches raw spots within our shredding cultural fabric to draw attention to greed, war, exploitation and the relentless process of needing to find our integral human selves:

> all the world's armies
>
> trained as cannon fodder
>
> they live to die

In these delicate and consummately-crafted pieces, one finds doors open to deep investigation of the moment and what it stands for in life's ever-shifting landscape. There is a stillness that the collection speaks from and to, a stillness that characterizes both the ukiyo-e and the haiku as art forms. Invested with extraordinary visual and tactile charm and an interesting Preface that throws light on the genesis and growth of the ukiyo-e in Japan, this book accomplishes a unique synthesis between two valuable Japanese artforms, bringing to a connoisseur-reader the unforgettable enchantment of both.

A Marginal Place in Poetry: Jaydeep Sarangi's *letters in lower case*

If she decides to come,
she may not.
If the forecast is, she will come,
she will not come.
Some months ago, her remote whisper
are the last rains falling in Kolkata.
Taking her on our side,
we keep white flowers on doorways.
We step into our smiles, longings,
absences, waiting in due time.
             - 'Waiting for Summer Rains in Kolkata'

Among the many things that poetry effortlessly accomplishes, is the renewal and repair of the everyday, the holding of a quiet, compassionate light to each day's dark, and the widening of the strong limbs of night to embrace all that is fallen and lost. Not all poetry has an axe to grind, a theorem to establish or a belief to popularize. It is possible for poems to be luminous and yet unseen until beckoned by the right moment of experience. Such poems seek nothing but to honour the soil of life that has birthed them and to return to it the nourishment it richly deserves.

In Jaydeep Sarangi's *letters in lower case* (Authorspress, 2022), one comes across a similar urge. The earth-brown cover of the book depicts a rain of alphabets -- the protagonist 'letters' in lower case. But these poems are equally letters in the sense of being epistles to the world -- letters that encapsulate an inordinate wisdom on its workings and teach us how to cohere with all its contradictions. The seventy-nine poems in this collection branch out to life in its myriad shades and teeming irreconcilabilities, documenting its steady, cyclical progression from despair to hope.

The title bespeaks much for these poems and for their particular stance towards the world. The lower case, here, is the case of the everyday traffic of writing and life. It is ungaudy, non-pompous and devoid totally of the slightest sense of self-importance. It is, however, at the same time, essential, integral, vital to existence and impossible to live without. By urging his poetry to stand tall and firm in lower case, the poet establishes the role of poetry as confidante and witness to life's routine transactions and its existential plurality and surprise. It also affirms poetry's marginality and the epistemological significance of the marginal position in the world.

The book is divided into three sections titled 'Laws of the Land', 'Gesture of Surrender' and 'The Window you Hold'. It is possible to read these sections in terms of the relationship of self and the world and to find them as explorations of 'Reality', 'Desire' and 'Possibility'. Poems in the first section engage themselves distinctly with the world as it is, squarely encountering its injustices. In most of Sarangi's poems, the currency of reality is raw description sans mantles of metaphor, sarcasm or idealism. His is an eye that takes keen pleasure in recording the world as it is rather than imaging it in accordance with visions it cannot or does not wish to live up to. Such embracing of life's is-ness can lead to a lack of coherence but it is precisely this experiential incoherence that marks Sarangi's oeuvre, his poems being distinct bridges between life and art.

In 'Road to Almora', the tranquillity and religio-spiritual significance of the Himalayas that lights up the poem is sternly contrasted with its last lines where "an old rickshaw puller perspires/ who never read Gandhi or Ambedkar/ history waved its delicate hands,/ the ride screamed to a stop." History, as Sarangi points out, can bypass the hapless, and social revolutions can leave many distressed lives unaffected. Life, however, goes on, settling into "a dreamless nonsensical sleep". In 'An Etymology of Gain', the poet eats the farmers' "tears, sweats, words" In 'A Love Poem for Jose Mujica', the inspiration is to describe the farmers' "fair green face/ And the pain of the world in one line."

In the second section of the book, poems surrender to desire and the heart's multi-layered longing for peace, stability, justice, reciprocal love and human faith. In 'Losses', the poet writes, "Losses are gains somewhere", convinced that the arithmetic of loss and gain is too wide to be mapped out entirely in relation to one's narrow self and circumstances. 'Someday you will suggest me to rain elsewhere/ What shall I do with my heart already given to you", states 'Morning', emphasizing a firm vision of the permanence of love in an ephemeral world. "Let me cry for myself/ my lost image in you" urges 'Light on My House' underlining the inalienable relationship between the self and the other. Throughout these poems, Sarangi's metaphors for emotions are both unusual and strongly resonant. Drawn out of the several recesses of day-to-day living, their force both charms and astounds. In 'Magic in Deep Breathings', for instance, age becomes "a conversation with faded colours". In 'Is there a Window?' the window becomes a metaphor for leisure and respite from a life continually duty-bound.

The third section of the book dwells on nostalgia and the possibility of a future that springs from the security of the past. A number of poems in this section are dedicated to family and friends, charting maps of a time that can be revived in memory alone. 'In Folders', for instance, documents a startling range of memories of place, sport festival, culture, literature and cuisine in tracing one's identity across time. 'A Poet's Unworthy Bio-note' metaphorically discusses the distances between biography and the summary note that professionally recounts it. "The present is/ a half-close door/ None can come and go/ without pushing the half-closed part", writes the poet in 'Dreams' establishing the nebulous connection between the conscious and the subconscious, between past and present, and reality and dreams.

The tone of *letters in lower case* is distinctly autumnal, its postmodernist conscience clear, and its postcolonial memory teeming with historical connections across temporal and cultural frames. The idea of homing, belonging and finding meaning in existence through relationships is a dominant theme within these poems as is the necessity of the self to committedly participate in the wider workings of the world. No human can or should be an island to oneself, these poems seem to assert. Rooted in a strong ethical consciousness that duly marks the presence of the socio-culturally underprivileged and dispossessed, Sarangi's poems valorise a marginal perspective on the world and evince extraordinary faith in the power of poetry and in the role of the poet as an architect of the future. In 'The Future is a Poet', Sarangi writes, "a poet is/ the arriving wind/ delayed without a fuss/ broke loose/ recalled." If poetry is the mending of the broken, the restoration of the ravaged and the invigoration of the weak, then the poet in society is akin to both the visionary and the healer.

Such existential healing, however, can be performed, as the poet asserts, not in the mainstream but only at the hems, the pockets and the interstices of self and culture. This repair and healing of the self on the one hand and of the rift between the self and the world on the other, is precisely the aesthetic and emotive function that *letters in lower case* performs. Its ideology, in its deep humanism and in advocating the role of love as the connecting force between all forms of being - human and non-human, and sentient and non-sentient, establishes these poems as wide-ranging anthems of selflessness, redemption and abiding contentment in the pleasures and potential of the human soul.

Spatialities of Reflection: Kashiana Singh's *Woman by the Door*

In *Ten Windows: How Great Poems Transform the World,* Jane Hirshfield writes, "Between the first word of a sentence and the second, a tiny expectation rises in its listener, requiring fulfilment. An article leans toward its noun, a noun toward its verb; a preposition tells us the mind is about to be moved in time or place." A similar terse magic animates, for me, the title of the book under consideration. Kashiana Singh's third collection of poems *Woman by the Door* (Apprentice House Press, 2022) offers, for the reader's contemplation, an interesting and intricate spatiality. Its poetic and political intentions put firmly on record by its unencumbered title and its neat, unambiguous cover, there are three well-articulated spaces that invite our attention here – the woman, the door and the threshold.

Having crystallized over the nine years since 2013 when the poet moved from India to the US, here are poems that encapsulate an intense and valuable experience of home-making and self-exploration between lived lands. The sixty-eight poems in the book are grouped into three different constellations themed 'Apertures', 'Portals' and

'Detours' that cartograph the spatial journeys that Kashiana undertakes and invites the reader to reflect on. The aperture of the mind regulates sensitivity, memory and wisdom. The portal prefigures identity by permitting or denying entries and exits. The detours determine the existential shape of our living through climaxes and crises.

The woman, throughout these poems, remains the nerve centre of the collection and a vital node of consciousness through whom ideas, ideologies, images and intuitions flow, circulate and sediment into knowledge. Kashiana's woman, as the reader will note, is not one. She is Everywoman who is committed to knowing herself through the world as well as an individual faced with an idiosyncratic existential challenge. But most significantly, as the cover indicates, she represents, for the poet, an ontological space for the experience of plural identities.

The diasporic vision in Kashiana locates in woman a site of multiple spatial cross-sections – biological, domestic, national, linguistic, cultural and more. Placed within these varying matrices of circumstances and relationships, the woman must negotiate home, self and the ways by which both are extended and sustained. Mothers, grandmothers, daughters, friends, aunts – all come to inhabit the ontological space of the poet's speculation on female selfhood in ways that are startling in their perspicacity.

In 'In the image of my mother', the mother becomes the first giver of meaning "with syntax/ of lunch boxes/ with storytelling/ under whirring fans/ with petulant warmth/ of a fresh casserole". In 'Becoming Planets', the various aspects of a woman's experiences and desires acquire cosmic proportions with the woman claiming herself as a planet of her own. One notes how gently the individual and the communal come together in these lines to weave a collage of women's collective strength in both celebration and mourning:

> I am a planet though; as every woman before
> I bleed myself hollow; I swallow my volcanoes
> I spin for all before me who were dwarfed
> I draw orbits around names of all our departed souls
> I weave a Kuiper belt with the fallen ringlets of my hair
> I gather our screams till they pierce through veins of these stars
> I repeat all of the above, I rotate, I revolve, I burn, I am born
> into the firmament above –

As a poet, Kashiana specializes in the meditative, her rare talent being to analyse the endodermis of things – facts, feelings, emotions and actions. The obvious, regular and mundane transform themselves through her poetic meditations into powerful loci for the interpretation of valuable cultural phenomena. In 'The Kitchen that is also a Monastery' for instance, the graphic description of the precise, geometric act of cutting vegetables brings together both pace and motion, metamorphosing the ordinary task of cooking into an extraordinary ritual of not just physical but also spiritual sustenance. In 'A Woman folding laundry', the marginal act of folding clothes acquires centre stage offering not only a new awareness of the tactile experience of each individual folded fabric but also bringing home the irksome magnitude of housework that, falling largely to women's share, passes unnoticed in the cultural reckoning of domestic labour.

In poems like 'Pagri' and 'Functions of a Saree', the poet reinterprets through cultural pride, memory and nostalgia, the value of cherished cultural traditions that embody connection with an absent community and an empowered sense of identity. Rampant in these poems is a relentless existential reassessment of knowledge and wisdom, of juggling between old-world and new-world knowledges and of walking through cultural and generation gaps to foster a sense of lineage across disrupted families and incomplete homes.

While Kashiana attempts a wide of range of free verse-forms in *Woman by the Door*, her favoured mode of expression here seems to be the interlinked haiku that offers both an intimate and a wide-ranging perspective on her subjects. The sharp images of the haiku along with its silent serenity expand the associative impact of her best poems to render them ornate perspectives on life's essential fragmentation and underlying unity.

The door and the threshold, the reader realizes, emerge as significant metaphorical spaces in her poetry. The door as a possibility signifies both promise and threat and the threshold exemplifies the idea of waiting in faith. Both become poignant locations for the poet to connect with the world and journey through the complex interior of representations. Kashiana's politics articulates a womanist inclusiveness, empathy and a brave acceptance of loss and pain. One encounters in her poems a consistent night-seeing and an overwhelming desire to question and negotiate with the darkness that borders our lives perennially.

In 'Dear Daughter, and Son', for instance, the process of moving house becomes a deep, emotive exploration of the space of transit for a mother since not all memories of her children can be dissociated from the house and neatly packed in a "square cardboard box". With tender but unforgiving psychological realism, the poet sculpts the contours of vacancy here – "hangers of shapes and sizes, limp/ on rods inside vacant closets that/ swallow the phrases caught inside/ walls of this house." At the conclusion of 'I Stopped Counting', another heart-wrenching poem, the poet articulates the burnt but defiant spirit of a victim of sexual abuse standing at the threshold of acceptance and strength through the image of a flaming pyre.

'Country', likewise becomes an impassioned address from the threshold to every nation that ignores its voices of sanity to transform into "the spitting fire of a trillion monarchs". "I am a lighthouse standing in watch" writes Kashiana here and the collection too, I would say, offers that profound and luminous sense of productive reflection as women globally wait by the door for an empathetic and meaningful future.

The Gospel of the Body: Nilim Kumar's *I'm Your Poet*

> I was about to write a poem
> digging the soil, pulling out words
> then the girl of soil who doesn't
> wear clothes arrived and said
> don't dig the soil
> don't dig the soil
> -   - 'A Poem's Body'

What is a poet made up of? If poetry is the life-blood of a poet and the essential soil of his heart, the reader, in order to establish intimacy with a book of poems, must ask what this soil is made up of. Is it layered by history, memory, desire or grief? Is it private or public, porous or impermeable? What hopes and fears have nurtured it? In the case of Nilim Kumar, one can say with conviction that the poet is intensely and accretively made up of the teeming world around him – his native land of Assam and his people who perfuse him with deep, overwhelming feeling.

To come to Nilim Kumar's *I'm Your Poet* (Red River, 2022) translated from the original Assamese by Dibyajyoti Sarma, one has to abandon the notion of the poet as conscious artist or as master of disguises, and return to the idea of the poet as inspired troubadour. Here is primarily a people's poet, someone who writes out of his fathomless love for humanity. Refusing to place the poet on an ontological elevation, Kumar, like Wordsworth, regards him as a man speaking to men. People are integral to Kumar's poetic vision, and for the humanist that he is, the focus on humanity overrules the love for land, the latter meaning nothing when estranged from its people.

In 'Save Poetry/ Save the Mice', the poet describes how, in order to meet a deadline for a magazine, he tried to secure the solace for writing poetry by doing "the most non-poetic thing" – "I put up a sign: / Busy Writing Poetry, Do Not Disturb". Nothing comes out of this endeavour for "In the house without people,/ the mice were the poems" and the poet concludes that "You cannot write poetry/ with these thoughts and images". To write poetry, Kumar needs in his world the density of people, a fact remarkably symbolized by the book's cover and its title. 'I'm Your Poet' is, thus, both acknowledgement and surrender – the acknowledgement that one's poetic task or destiny lies mired with one's people, and a surrender to public estimate, however harsh or unjust it might be. In 'Tree of Love', for instance, the world climbs the tree of love in the poet's heart "with a machete" cutting down everything till only "the roots remain" but this does not defeat the poet's resolve to offer love to his people:

> this time, I'll grow underground,
> I'll grow underground
> you're all invited,
> come again

"For me, poetry is the language that facilitates conversation between life and the world. There is no place for the artificial here," states Kumar in a conversation with Anindita Kar. His poems bespeak intensity, authenticity, great depth of feeling, unbridled lyricism, and a strong humanist predilection. There's a sharp earthiness in these poems -- a scent of sun, soil, sweat, tears, rain and blood that connect man to man. Poetry, for Kumar, is intrinsically a social act by which the poet and his people enter into a commune, and the joys, sorrows, aspirations and dread of his fellowmen become his own, pining for expression. Here is a shared vision of the world, an aspiration for common good, and a desire to remedy the pain of others by reminding them of the gifts of life – beauty, human connection and love, through poems that Subodh Sarkar finds "as life-giving as a plateful of rice".

"Poets," writes Subodh Sarkar, "have always found a thrill in the quest of good people. There are times when the way is lost. But the search for human goodness has not diminished in poetry. There is no poet in the world who has not, in his own unique way, dived into the depths of the world looking for a good man. Nilim Kumar has been doing the same." The nearly hundred poems in this collection are an evocative testimony of the poet's journey with and through his people, an attempt to voice the angst of his times, and to relentlessly search for sources of succour and shared vitality, envisaging for himself the same role as he does for sunshine in his poem 'Sunshine':

> Sunshine descends not just for the woman.
> It comes down for everyone.
> It opens its arms for the people.
> Through people's skins, through
> their skins and bones, Sunshine wants
> to reach for people's hearts.

When does a poem become a poem? When it has gone through the heart's grist, Kumar would say, poetry recording for him "the language of the human heart". One is, indeed, moved by the wide range of feeling that these poems effectively handle – love, friendship, family, the innocence and nostalgia of childhood, the striking lust of adolescence, the enigma of youth, the betrayal of old age, and the sharp sting of loss at any age whatsoever. There is no observation for Kumar that is also not emotive, no emotive apprehension that is also not aesthetic, and no aesthetic perception which is also not sensual. This does not imply a dismissal of rationality but the privileging of a different kind of logic that places intuition and subjectivity at the centre of his vision. Passion is the pen of Kumar's verse. Nothing that does not touch his soul can be a part of his poetic canvas about which there is nothing private or veiled. The self that he writes is essentially a public self whose myriad emotions he explores with unabashed authenticity and overwhelming devotion.

Given Kumar's thrust on the human, there is little wonder that these poems engage in an intimate relationship with the human body. True to his training as a doctor, corporeality becomes integral to Kumar's poetic praxis, a fundamental source of both being and knowledge. For Kumar, there is nothing ignominious about the body's essential humanity and vulnerability. Not merely a physical entity but an intensely social and political site for experience, communication and belonging, it is the body that gives pain and "pleasure to another body", gives "birth to another body", and is responsible for honour and shame ('Memoir'). The body, whether it is that of the mother ('Carry Me Again in Your Womb'), the grandmother ('Grandmother'), the beloved ('Pregnant') , the servant boy ('Childhood') the girl at puberty, ('Puberty') or whether it belongs to Radha, Ruby Gupta, Achina, Kamala Konwari,

Sukhpaa, Nandini or to women in a painting, becomes central to both the ontology and the epistemology of these poems. For a poet as devoted to the gospel of the body as Kumar is, the celebration of its beauty through love becomes the prayer and salvation of poetry.

Love becomes a human practice in *I'm Your Poet*, therapeutic and resurrective in lightening the burden of life's essential absurdity – this living "just to spend the hours" which have "No meaning. No meaning." ('Cohabitation'). A flair for the narrative marks many of these poems, Kumar's primary urge being anecdotal and often surreally so. Translated with as great a passion as engendered the original poems, this collection that richly infuses Indian English with the deft and fluid syntactical structures of the Assamese language and with an extraordinary range of sensuous and sensual images drawn from its local flora and fauna, constitutes a timeless gift for readers of English, buttressing Nilim Kumar's status as one of the most significant poets of our time.

Where Poetry Meets Enigma: Oindri Sengupta's *After the Fall of a Cloud*

As I begin Oindri Sengupta's *After the Fall of a Cloud* (Hawakal Publishers, 2022), the title of the book meets me half-way. A sense of disturbance in my mind lurks around the phrase 'after the fall' evoking connotations of finality beyond resurrection. The vibrant blue cover, however, seems to offer an assurance of optimism, a clear flag of the victory of life over death. That the poet is talking of the fall of a cloud faintly surprises for clouds, when they fall, transform into rain. I begin to smell 'fall', therefore, for biblical undertones and mind-hunt for metaphorical possibilities - betrayal, loss, death, exile. It is not till I arrive at the sixth poem in the collection that I get a clue:

> I had the vision of a land where
> love would fall from the fading moon
> to give birth to another
> that comes only when the sky dreams
> after the fall of a cloud.

The sky dreaming after the fall/departure/absence of a cloud it had loved/held/embraced confirms my train of thoughts. The poem is significantly called 'Love – A Difficulty' and begins with "Love is another difficulty". That 'another' is faintly suggestive of the pervasive dissonances of life. A few poems later, in 'Smells like Sea', the poet chances to focus on the idea of 'difficult'. "Staying alive is difficult," the poem states, and goes on to ask:

> What does difficult mean to you?
> Does it mean you cannot breathe?
> Or do you not remember that you are alive?

One instantly realizes that there is more here than meets the eye and what is said is only a reductive preface to the great deal that remains unsaid.

Reading the 64 poems in this book comes across as a puzzle, a deep enigma whose roots are difficult to trace. The sensuousness of the collection is undeniable. Beginning from the very first poem, wave after wave of tactile images make their way to the reader. Sight, sound, touch, taste and smell are all engaged participants here. Colours, for instance, play vibrantly, sometimes wildly in these poems like "the coloured fever of a rainbow" ('The Nameless') In 'Colours', Sengupta writes, "Red sky is your wings/ that lie over the dawns and my green breasts." In 'Voices of Shadows', "She speaks the language of the stars/ and her silver hair is as blue as mine".

Sengupta's canvas is vitally etched with nature's wealth – with mountains, forests, seas and rivers that play upon days and nights with their iridescence and their quiet, unseen activities. Vivid and appealing as this landscape is, one cannot help noticing that it is immune to even the slightest change. Days, nights and seasons may arrive here in succession but such temporal divisions hold no meaning for both this poetic universe and the consciousness that creates it. Both remain still and unchanging, the only motion in these poems being the acrobatics of reflective connections. In 'Sunlight on the Hills', the poet says, "A little night with hundred daffodils/ is all you need to recreate/ a sunlight on the hills." The idea of night as an ingredient for sunlight astounds as does the sentence "I have given up dreams,/ to borrow one hundred light years of life/ from your nights." ('Blood and Dreams') Such leaps of reflection continue in poem after poem with nouns swaying into adjectives that transform into verbs with the swiftness of water. The emotional tenor, however, remains constant in its melancholia and in the mystery of an inscrutable landscape unyielding its secrets to the reader.

A sense of closetedness looms large over this volume with the wider world of reality and experience deliberately kept out of its poetic canvas. Apart from the sudden concrete glimpse of a mother, a son, or a friend, there are no humans to be found in these lines except as abstract addressees. There are no relationships here except those of longing, no stories except those of seeking in time and timelessness. Memories abide but even these must be interpreted according to the emotional dynamics of the present. In all, one confronts here, a deeply closeted world, carefully constructed like a prism to reflect the meanderings of the mind rather than concrete objective reality.

In determinedly steering away from objectivity, the poems gain, sometimes, in ambiguity and enigma. The pace of the collection remains steady but the emotional logic can baffle the reader at times. In "all the kites in the sky/ dropped like the petals of night" ('Voices of Shadows'), one wonders what 'kites' could refer to. Bereft of people, this landscape can only, anachronistically, host paper kites. The possibility of birds of prey dropping like petals is sustainable but jarring. The two ideas combined with the possibility of the kites as metaphor lends a density to the interpretation that interferes with its fluidity. In "Hands of clay make stones of hunger/ to write over the sunbeams - / a desolate thunder of words" ('When All is Lost'), the intense emotional logic baffles again. There is a kind of magic realism at play here blending the possible and the impossible in the deep interests of emotive truth. The pathway of associations is difficult to follow at times but though the logic evades, the overarching lyricism of these compositions is, in no way, compromised.

The persona that characterizes these poems and is, in turn, characterized by them, is as enigmatic as the landscape that breathes here. In 'Strange Meetings', Sengupta writes, "We meet as strangers/ in this island of nowhere,/ playing merry-go-round/ with our masked identities." Each poem in this book presents itself to me as a mask where the ornate play of words permits expression through concealment and vice-versa. In 'Falling Leaves', the speaker is aware of being "watched" and "judged" till "my hands are dyed with blood,/ and I lie/ in this land of dead rivers." If confession must undergo such censorship, Sengupta prefers to play dexterously with language and to dismantle its very frames of reference. She jumbles up word classes, allows them to run into each other like colours and uses them, kaleidoscopically, to create an astounding self-referential linguistic spectacle. A deft artist, she hides herself behind words and attempts to find catharsis in the act of building poems around her as impenetrable fortress that can be vanquished only through emotional resonance and poetic empathy.

An ornate linguistic weave, *After the Fall of a Cloud*

is a narrative of emotional documentation that will make its way into the minds and hearts of readers who, aware of life's conflicting and irreconcilable urges, seek no lasting philosophical solutions but only the assurance of provisional peace.

The Place of Memory/The Memory of Place: Pramila Venkateswaran's

We are Not a Museum

A certain sublimity rises from the page to take charge of your senses as you step into the landscape of Pramila Venkateswaran's eighth collection of poems, *We Are Not a Museum* (Finishing Line Press, 2022). The fine latticework of sentiment and language beckons you in every poem here, inviting you to advance into its mystery. The light is mellow gold, the quietness, sepia, and the voice, vintage through and through. Luxuriating in the book's expansive calm, you wish to know where you are. Answers rush to you as waves to the shore and there is no way you can choose between one answer and another. You let them all kiss your curiosity and gently recede, surrendering yourself to the metaphysics of the question.

We Are Not a Museum is certainly, as its subtitle states, about the Jews of Kochi and the city of Kochi itself, but it is also, equally, about the place of memory, about memory as place, and about the memories of a community acquired by being-in-place. Thematically intrinsic to this book are the idea of home, the making of a self/hood, the palimpsest of identity, the amnesia of history, and the necessity of commemoration as a political act within the rampant socio-cultural practices of erasure of minority groups across the world today, with the result that a defiant ethical urge to establish a just historical narrative for memory, deeply animates these poems.

The Jews of Kochi constitute the oldest of the five groups of Jews in India believed, by many, to have set foot on the Southwestern Malabar coast as merchants of the Hebrew king, Solomon in the 10th century BC. In recorded history, Judaism is the first foreign religion to have arrived in India, finding and making a safe and distinct place for itself on the country's syncretic soil. Later, in the 16th century, another wave of Sephardi Jews is supposed to have entered Malabar from Iberia, fleeing the Spanish and Portuguese Inquisitions. Known more popularly as the Paradesi Jews or Foreign Jews, they first made the ancient port of Cranganore and later, after its silting, the port of Kochi or Cochin as it was known until 1996, their home.

Embracing wholeheartedly the Malayalam language and using Hebrew only for religious purposes, the Jews adapted themselves to their new homeland with grit, gusto, resilience, and faith, and though numerically, they were never a very large group, they soon established a significant cultural presence within their local community via architectural, artistic, culinary, sartorial, religious and spiritual influences. In the economic and political life of Kerala also, the role of the Jews remained noteworthy. Their industry, mercantile capital, navigational expertise, ability to mobilize resources and establish cross-oceanic Semitic networks for the circulation of spices and other commodities between the Indian Ocean and the Mediterranean, were of great significance to the local rulers who frequently relied on the Jews to meet much of their emergency and wartime expenses.

The Jews of Kochi, thus, flourished for almost two thousand years, under the patronage of the local rulers, their settlements and synagogues becoming valuable cultural texts within Kerala's changing cityscape, and the nuclei around which the trade and commerce of its local markets constellated. However, deteriorating economic opportunities and the decline in their socio-economic status after the independence of India in 1947, and the historical simultaneity of the birth of their historic homeland of Israel as a nation in 1948, led to an exodus of the Jews from Kerala. Today, the community has less than a handful of members, and its cemeteries and synagogues have all fallen into decay, the Paradesi synagogue being the only one with regular religious congregations on its premises. Some synagogues have been vandalized, some sold, some adapted as warehouses or shops, two having been converted into museums to showcase the heritage of the Jewish community.

The title of Pramila Venkateswaran's distilled collection of forty poems, *We Are Not a Museum*, a glorious and heartfelt tribute to the Jewish past and present of Kochi, derives, perhaps, from a cultural activist impetus to decry the museumization of the Jews by establishing a strong counter-narrative of their vital, breathing and throbbing presence within the historical social fabric. It is essential to note the pronoun 'we' in the title, a key to the identity of kinship that the speaker of these poems upholds. When one recalls Venkateswaran's own Tamil Brahman identity, her philosophical and epistemological identification with the Jews by erasing the self/other boundary and accomplishing a merging of subjectivity, throws light on an important ideological aspiration of the book – the mnemonic restoration of cultural plurality and of India's (now highly threatened) syncretic multiculturalism. Written from the Indian diaspora, Venkateswaran's observations on identity also raise valuable questions about the existential nature of global migrations, the perpetual encounter between the present and the past, the un/reliability of history, the politics of official memory, and the urgent need to establish alternate personal and public archives of narrative remembering.

"Coming is always arduous/ —mountains, near-death escapades/ until you chalk a square space/ and call it home," begins the first poem of the collection, 'Exile' that commemorates the coming of the Jews to Malabar amidst "Arabs/ Christians, Syrian Christians/ Hindus and Buddhists on/ this Keral land divinely blessed" ('Gifting and Receiving') In the form of short historical vignettes and in a language that is, both, highly emotive and economic in its tight suggestiveness, these poems document the entire 2000 year history of the Jews of Kochi. In the narrative of arrival in 'The Long Journey', one notes startling parallels to the narratives of the refugees of the Partition in India, their urgent wrapping up of home by bundling

> ...everything they owned:
> two skirts, two blouses, a loaf of bread, dried
> olives, figs, some meat,
> a square cloth, two bowls,
> Joseph's robe, the family Bible,
> and a small sack of earth
> to remind them where they came
> from.

One notes, with wonder, Venkateswaran's remarkable ventriloquism in these poems as she assumes, throughout the book, a range of voices – of the first-generation migrant

Jews, of the locals who welcomed them, of the second and third generations of Jews in Kochi, of those who emigrated to Israel, and finally, her own. 'Chorus: At the Palace of the Raja of Cochin' describes how the Jews must have appeared to the local populace – "speaking a tongue we have not heard before" but "there is grace in their speech". 'Esther Hosts her Sisters in Kochi Synagogue' offers an eloquent description of the Jews adapting their socio-religious traditions to local customs and practices, thus fostering a version of Judaism that seamlessly blended with Kerala's multi-ethnic cultural terrain: "In full-sleeved churidhar kameez she smiles like Kochi harbor/ At her sisters who've come from deserts bruised orange." Written loosely in the ghazal form, the use of the radif 'orange' invokes a host of symbolic associations in every couplet – of exile, assimilation, toil, globalized cultural homogenisation, the most telling being "how violent thoughts manifest in orange" -- an unignorable reminder of the rising right-wing violence in India in the service of saffronism and purism. 'Naming' voices the dream of one generation of Jews for a more empowered next generation as the speaker, in choosing a name for a daughter, wants to make a choice that is sufficiently modern and yet, proudly connected to their ethnic roots: "I want a name with currency, modern./ Daughter with heft. Her words will move worlds./ I want my mol to be a presence/ no one will forget. So Golda it will be."

There is an abundance of ethnographic detail here -- details of cuisine "fish kozhambu, rice and appam" ('Dear Papa'), religious services to mark gratitude for "the honey of life" ('Evening Song') , Jewish mythology, the Jewish graves above the ground "in a large field—mound after mound—/As if symmetry helps us swallow/ the unbearable." (Cemetery), and so on. The city of Kochi acquires, through such details, an almost tangible presence in the reader's imagination with its "comfort of succor/ among the tumult of the market, in the lazy/ rocking of the boats on dreamy water".

The spirit of syncretism powerfully underlines the book's narrative. 'Torah Scrolls' recalls how the gold crowns on the filigreed cylinders that held the sacred Torah scrolls in a synagogue, were a gift from the local Raja of Travancore "for he knew the worth/ of guarding the sacred store". 'The Clock Tower' describes the 45 feet tall clock tower that was erected in 1760 next to the Paradesi synagogue in Mattanchery by a Jewish businessman, its unique feature being its four faces with numerals written in Hebrew, Arabic, Roman, and Malayalam – an imposing architectural assertion of Kochi's composite cultural heritage.

Deftly watermarking this collection is the metaphor of journey, a symbolic narrative acknowledgement of the multiple migrations, physical and psychological, of the Jews. Poems like 'Desert Experiment', 'History', 'Movement', and 'Immigrating to Israel' conjure the decline of the Jewish community in Kochi as a result of unfavourable economic conditions in India and their mass emigration to Israel - "As the land that was promised took more than it was offered,/ my grandchildren flew to the Negev" ('Desert Experiment'). In 'Our Days Are Like Passing Shadows' and 'Field Trip', those who choose to stay behind remain conscious of deepening decadence and approaching cessation. Almost every poem in the book registers an acute awareness of movement, of arrivals and departures, of 'to' and 'from', each of them continually changing physical places till they merge into the metaphysical:

Soon they will stop looking

back.
Just like in the afterlife, no one
says, "Oh, I want to go back,"
knowing full well the passage will be the same:
shuffling one's way to the afterlife. ('History')

"We are racing against /time, intone anthropologists, archiving every / letter and coin, for memory is unreliable," states the poet in the eponymous poem 'We are Not a Museum', fully conscious that such archiving is not enough until we summon ethics and empathy to the entire cultural memory project. It is in this deeply existential dimension that *We Are Not a Museum* refuses to be about only Jews or Kochi and becomes both requiem and anthem in and for a globalized world order where institutionalized erasure of minorities is the only way through which ideological fanaticism can sustain itself.

In its resurrection of place and memory, *We Are Not a Museum*, thus, becomes a powerful *sthalapurana* for the city of Kochi and the life of the Jews in it. Its eyes penetrate deep into the past, its ears are sharp, and in its cadence is a spiritual majesty that befits the profundity of its project. To have the content of *We Are Not a Museum* put together as historical nonfiction would have been admirable but in poetry, its vision, range and profound lyricism magically astound. The narrative, with its rhythmic juxtaposition of several temporal frames, offers a sense of linearity as well as circularity, both dimensions being integral to historical understanding. There is a grace in the narration that refuses to surrender to the exigencies of history, its poise being an aesthetic symbol of the resilience of minorities globally, and a reminder of how, after everything is lost, the story remains to become a vital strategy of reclamation.

Tracing a Tiger: Sukrita Paul Kumar's *Vanishing Words*

To miss making one's way through Sukrita Paul Kumar's *Vanishing Words* (Hawakal Publishers, 2022) and to forgo being absorbed into the vortex of its supraconscious stillness would be, for any reader of poetry, a serious deprivation. Many-layered, teasing in its apparent simplicity, and haunting in its profundity, this slim collection of thirty-four poems interspersed with artwork by the poet herself, is dedicated to "all those who are struggling to survive the onslaught of disease and the loss of dear ones in the recent times".

Taking her cue from the dedication, the reader opens the book to reach out for companionship and solace. What awaits her, however, is a dense transformative experience marked by the realization of the immateriality of life, the impossibility of death and the inherent mutability of all forms of being – physical, psychological and emotional.

"Why would the tiger of silence not leave/ any pug marks behind in the forest of words?" muses Sukrita. This, one surmises, is no catechism but an apposite hypothesis to begin a new poetic exploration. An established, accomplished and widely recognized poet, Sukrita is no stranger to the "forest of words". A committed inhabitant of it, she is, rather, on a different trail this time, her poetry being a determined attempt to seek out these pug marks of silence from the heart of the world's cacophony.

The task that the poet sets herself to, here, is hardly easy and has, only rarely, been accomplished in poetry. In search of a poetic diction that seeks to select "words that cancel all noise in themselves,/ such that pulsate in echoes of meaning and then/ vanish into colourless space -/ past sound beyond meaning", *Vanishing Words* grows or rather condenses into a dissertation and testament on the fine, subtle and elusive spaces between silence and speech, between word and wordlessness, between inertness and stillness, and between emptiness and void.

The theme of this collection is wide-ranging. Identity, nostalgia, deep contemplation, interconnectedness of the natural and human worlds, social evils, life, death, art – all and more, manifest themselves in these poems with a grace that is quiet, unassertive, and yet memorably poignant. Note, for instance, the following line from 'Little Ones' -

Children play
with toys
adults with their
conscience.
or these from 'Game of Life':
I will not let my palm betray me
I have shut its big mouth
With a line tattooed on it
I can hoodwink the palmist

A dazzling painter, Sukrita fluidly transacts between poetry and painting, heavily cross-borrowing ideas and methods, and cross-fertilizing her work in both genres of art. One would be astounded to observe her consistent play of surface and depth in both her poems and artwork in this collection. In 'On the Dal at Srinagar', surfaces belie depths and on the tranquil water of the lake, the observer's visage becomes "a cubist's work/ of art/ yellow, red, green,/ blue and even bits of white/ and purple,/ joined together with/ affection, love, attachments/ likes and dislikes." A whole emotional geography comes alive, here, in colour and motion, necessitating and defying the need to order, arrange or simplify.

Animated by her painter's consciousness, her images are terse, pictorial and at the same time, both concrete and abstract. In 'Affirmation', the fertility of "nothingness" is imaged as "the complete circular wetness/ out of/ a bubble exploded/ on a dry, blank slate." 'Above the Ground' describes prayers as lying in "unclosed parenthesis/ suspended in the/ firmament". 'Unwarranted Exit' which pays a moving tribute to the Gorakhpur hospital tragedy, sharply concretizes and thereby, urgently humanizes the shapelessness and epistemological neutrality of statistical data:

> Numbers don't matter
> Till they become razors
> The edges rubbing into the heart
> Sending shards of pain
> And the tunnel to death widening
> for the rising numbers to enter

There is, throughout Sukrita's canvas, a ceaseless seeking for connection – across temporalities, memories, ontologies, spatialities and creative routes. Ecological, philosophical, spiritual and deeply humanitarian, these connections make for a close-knit and intense experience of earth-bondedness. In 'One and All' she writes:

> The same hunger
> The same pangs
> Connect us all
> When the distance between
> Food and self
> Is not covered.

'The Chosen One' is a moving description of a chestnut tree struck by lightning – "The soul/ as if/ pulled out". The tree, however, is not alone in its fall for its tragedy has rendered "the monkeys of Summerhill/ as if/ motherless", its chestnuts no longer available to satiate their hunger. In 'Of Gaddi(s) and Goats', the silken warmth of the pashm fabric becomes a transplanetary manifestation of emotional nourishment:

> In its heat you may not cook eggs
> Nor will its lightness give you wings
> But what you wrap around yourself
> Are the dense clouds trapped in the Arctic
> Ready to rain on separation
> Or melt into sprightly rivers in its warmth.

In poems like 'With My Chinar Again', 'Colour that Bleeds' and 'Arrival at Paris', Sukrita connects continents, cultures, ideologies, dreams and aspirations through the celebration of art and artists – Toni Morrison, Simone de Beauvoir, Sylvia Plath, Ismat Chughtai, Lal Ded, the Ajanta Caves and more. In 'Cosmic Connections', death becomes an illusion and a doorway to a deeper affirmation of love – "Intergenerational networks/ Through shared memories".

However, the piece that stands out for me in this thoroughly impressive collection is its longest and concluding poem – 'Crows are Our Ancestors'. A brilliant display of bravura, the poem showcases Sukrita at her ardent, satirical and sinewy best. Divided into eight sections, here is an intricate acrobatics of ideas that connotatively link the crow as signifier to biography, metaphysics, culture, lineage, minority status, dissent, violence, vulnerability, resilience and permanence. A remarkable energy characterizes the poem as significations elegantly glide, strike, ricochet and bounce off each other leading to the manifestation of a cumulative and immensely symbolic whole that is ultimately far greater than the sum of its parts:

> No spirit in the body
> No wind in the wings
> The carcass lies in the centre

The Buddha and present or absent paths are frequent images in these poems as the poet moves through unchartered territories of thought, feeling and experience, relying solely upon her own intuition and instinct. Tracing the pug marks of the tiger of silence being her whole inspiration and ambition, her destination is the journey. The act of creation alone can be redemptive and liberate her from the "cross nailed by/ Unborn poems, aborted paintings/ Neither living/ Nor dead" and towards this, she strives with undeterred faith and an open soul.

As I close the book, its title and cover gather greater significance. Black and white, it strikes me, is a dominant theme of the collection, accentuated by the black and white paintings that contextualize and contour its poems. Symbolic of the play of darkness and light, life and death, truth and illusion, sound and silence, ephemerality and permanence and infinitely more, black and white also represent, in these poems, a cosmic interweaving of existence with awareness.

The cover that suggestively marks black against white

signifying both motion and immobility, leaves me in awe of its spatial dynamics and of the daunting project of creatively pursuing a silent tiger that Sukrita has not only taken up but accomplished with Blakean fervour. The compression, precision, lightness and luminosity of these poems is undeniable. There is, in them, a simplicity, intensity and finesse that characterizes classical Eastern forms like the haiku and the tanka. The tiger of silence having entered your mind once, the vanishing act is completely mastered. No doubt then that *Vanishing Words* will leave you both satiated and wistful for a long time to come.

Grief as Vestibule: Vinita Agrawal's *The Natural Language of Grief*

Of all emotions that accompany and inhabit sentience, that of grief is, perhaps, the toughest to engage with. An intimately subjective response to an objective loss, the intensity and profundity of an individual's grief can be hard to fathom. How does one grieve? Where does grieving begin and, if at all, conclude? Is it personal or communal? How can grief be communicated? How does it relate to life and the world at large? These are not easy questions to take up and yet, it is important to embark on a sound theory of grief in order to perfect its practice and to transform the experience of grieving into a corridor through which one enters a world that is significantly wider, more expansive and far more meaningful.

Vinita Agrawal's fifth collection of poems *The Natural Language of Grief* (Proverse Hong Kong, 2022) courageously confronts each of these challenging interrogations as it sets out to cartograph the dense, mosaic, and affectively charged territory of the grieving mind. The fifty-six distinct yet emotively hyperlinked poems in this book look at grief from multiple vantage points, contexturing a cathartic manual, both, for the close understanding of grief and for the act of grieving in a world too brittle and occupied to acknowledge the fullness of grief's vacancy.

The poems in this book, as the writer states, are "crepuscular – looking at dimness", their entire motivation being to illumine in speech those concealed seams of experience through which life's losses are suffered, accounted for, and redeemed in and through memory. Language constitutes a vital thematic motif within the collection, the object of these poems being both to give grief tongue (expression) and to find a tongue (language) appropriate for the articulation of grief.

Human acknowledgement of the therapeutic need to put grief to words is as old as life itself, the need for lamentation being as existential and archetypal as the urge for celebration. However, the postmodern world we live in is characterized by a glaring absence of a register of grief. The traditionally cultivated and inherited language of mourning, so recognizable and accessible to our ancestors, having been irrevocably lost today, the result is a decapacitating emotional vacuum that can be filled only by painstakingly building up a new linguistic register. Agrawal's poems attempt to forge this much-needed language by delving deep into the recesses of the human mind and seeking a poetic warp that can best encapsulate the diversity and complexity of mourning as both noun and verb.

What is equally noteworthy, here, is Agrawal's staunch insistence on the philosophical necessity to mourn, given the undeniable despair of our times. The act of mourning entails not only an acceptance of loss but also the admission of the value of what has been lost. In a post-truth world where loss is the norm, the act of objective evaluation of worth stands so completely eroded that no loss is acknowledged as impoverishment and the act of mourning itself is deemed extraneous. Agrawal offers an intervention to this defeating narrative of cultural devaluation of loss by focusing on the dynamics of grieving and establishing the negotiation of grief as vital to living.

Grief in these poems, as the reader realizes, can be intensely personal. There is the loss of parents – "the way every 2nd of July has been since then/ -- rain drenched" ('Dear Mother'); the having to deal with each element of the loss in a piecemeal fashion as one gradually comes to terms with terminal illness in a loved one – "this in your fourth stage/ when the doctors say/ you might find it hard to breathe" (*'Gunjiyas'*), practically experiences the lack of compassion in our healthcare system – "I rushed across hospitals for changes,/ facing the arrogance of these places./ The helplessness, the bone weariness." ('Dear Mother'), and lives with the consistent awareness of life inching closer to death – "Togetherness is so fragile. For dinner/ I eat scrambled nights shoving them around/ the plate of solitude." ('Grieving')

The act of bidding a ritualistic farewell from life to those we have deeply loved and the process of learning to live with their absence on a daily basis can make grief seem like war with oneself. "Don't I know how short patience is with grief?" exclaims the poet in 'Grieving'. Wisdom, however, lies, neither in running away from grief nor in deferring its acknowledgement but in the acceptance of the experience of impoverishment with fortitude, and the exploration of what such ordained impoverishment and wilful fortitude can teach one about life – "Separation/ is a cardinal direction./ A compass./ Opposite direction from the east./ The direction in which the sun sets." ('Separation').

It is, however, compelling to note that loss, in these poems, refuses to be self-centred or narcissistically melodramatic, reaching out, empathetically and tirelessly, to join forces with a collective, communal archive of deprivation. At the cornerstone of Agrawal's poetics is the firm desire to establish a communion between the human and nonhuman worlds and to consistently discover larger frames for the emotion and experience of grief. Thus, 'A Poem Born From Guilt' mourns not only the death of a pet parrot but also the temporal self that had expected the bird "to enjoy the cage/ enjoy his enclosure in my home/ enjoy his lavish pantry". Similarly, in 'Pelt, Fur and Chamois', "the soundless slickness of knives./ Flesh removed by hand. The soaking, liming,/ machining. Unhairing, degreasing, desalting" rears its head as a mindless monstrosity against the breeze that poignantly "ruffles the pelt, fur and chamois wherever it's worn/ like a blind grandfather feeling his children with his hands./ Like it failed to save a precious thing."

The experiences of the pandemic in which "the air, tight like a second skin,/ overstretched with my fears" ('Pandemic') assume another vital reference point for the consolidation of these poems. With great subtlety and finesse, Agrawal brings out, in this collection, the various codes of living that the pandemic has given new meaning to - isolation, distancing, intimacy, privilege, homelessness, courage, empowerment and the triumph of hope. "Proximity is lethal/ distance, benign", she writes in 'Atom in a Language Ordinary'. All three poems -'Migrant, Exodus', 'Jeeta Madkami' and 'The Walk of Hunger'- are moving takes on the crisis of the migrant workers whose long walk home is "a withdrawal from impoverishment,/ Reflex against singeing", undertaken in the full knowledge that "this walk/ is about another kind of hunger;/ the hunger for roots and familiarity/ a circle where he's at the core, not periphery."

The book begins with the understanding of waiting as "a boat on the shore/ or an urn of warm ashes/ tied to a tree or a clothesline" ('I Tell The River That I Shall Pray Again') and concludes with "Yellowed leaves of pain and tyrannies of love" and "tender feelings, gentler than a fawn" lying "in stock after festive spring has gone" ('What Lies in Stock') thus, establishing one full circle of realization that grief is neither extraordinary nor exclusive but an inescapable part of each day's fabric and must be met with acceptance, healing and faith.

Agrawal's images are poignant and her metaphors profound, her language reaching incessantly for a keen philosophical maturity. The deep wisdom in these poems is undeniable as is their urge to put every knowledge to test through the grid of experience. Abundant in its lyricism, the pace of this collection is as contemplative and unhurried as its search for clarity and calm.

Adjudged the winner of the Proverse Prize 2021, *The Natural Language of Grief* is an incantatory exploration of the polysemic language of grief that is also profusely polyphonic in its range of intonations and experiences. Inviting us to question our imperviousness and indifference to the fraying of everyday, and teaching us to redraw our notions of self and sorrow, the vestibular poems in this book, in asserting human fragility and reiterating the indispensable need to establish a truce with pain, perform the act of healing through speech on behalf of an entire generation that is untutored in the language of mourning.

A Case for the Body: Kuhu Joshi's *My Body Didn't Come Before Me*

The body is a text, writing and written on. As much of this text is 'given' as it is 'fashioned', its meaning continually negotiated at the intersections of self, society, and culture. Thoroughly personal, the body cannot, at the same time, escape from being spectacularly public because in its corporeality, it constantly responds to the material and metaphysical dimensions of the world around it. A body is being, becoming, possession, as also performance. It is, at the same time, uncertainty, liability, incarceration, and an alibi against everything that we might wish it to be.

In Kuhu Joshi's slim collection of thirty-five poems titled *My Body Didn't Come Before Me* (Speaking Tiger, 2023), the problematic of the body is placed at the centre of poetic inquiry. The crisp and categorical title catches the readers' attention first and in many ways, the cover offers a brilliant paratext to the ideas in this book as it evocatively underlines a conversation between girlhood, body, nature, and form.

We are never merely inhabitants of our bodies but also bear responsibility for our embodiment. The question of identity is, to a great extent, framed by questions of embodiment, and the conformity of the body to established cultural codes. Such conformity, however, is a sheer travesty of nature. Kuhu Joshi's poems chart the development and growth of selfhood through severe scoliosis or spinal deformity and the experience of alienation that gathers around it led by societal conventions of normalcy.

Central to these poems is a conflict between embodiment and selfhood, and the numerous ways in which socio-cultural codes of accomplishment, lifestyle, and beauty dictate the need for possessing the 'perfect' body. Often, ideas of romance and scripts of love and longing also reiterate the same narrative, rendering desire and its fulfilment both difficult and transgressive. This book is an ardent statement of such experiences of otherness and an activist desire to dismiss them into the idea of individuality or selfhood.

Joshi's poems delineate subtle contradictions between the body-as-construct and the body-as-experience with insight, freshness, and candour. There is little sentimentality in these pages, almost no lamentations of victimhood, and hardly any regret for life as it has been or is. But in their abrupt matter-of-factness and remarkable economy of expression, these poems manage to communicate a startling range of emotions – pain, fear, shame, depression, self-loathing, forbearance, and self-confidence.

The collection, interestingly, begins with 'I tell myself I am beautiful', a poem that on the page curves itself like a scoliotic spine: "...And I tell myself/ I am beautiful/ so I do not feel the need/ to be normal. I tell myself/ I am beautiful/ so I do not feel the need/ to be something I am not." The poem offers a convergence of several themes that will underlie the book – embodiment, normalcy, beauty, de/form/ity, narrativization, and selfhood.

Despite the grand diversity of bodies that inhabit this world and the numerous modes of embodiment, stereotypes of normalcy rule our everyday lives to such an extent that even the slightest deviation from the norm sparks reactions that inject within us feelings of otherness. Such narratives of otherness can only be combated through self-fashioned narratives of beauty, experience, identification and identity.

The body at the centre of these poems is a body consistently othered by medical discourse. But it is also, and with equal tenacity, a female body that through its girlhood, adolescence, pubescence and growth, must bear the implications of this otherness in more ways than one with the result that everyday narratives of friendship, safety, love, and desire are complicated in their enunciation. In 'The girl with a rod', one of the most tender poems in the collection, the subtle yet dramatic inter-gender confrontation between two adolescents raises several questions on normalcy, vulnerability, and comfort in social spaces – here, the seemingly innocuous space of a school bus.

And yet, the speaker in these poems acknowledges that when it comes to another scoliotic body, her own gaze is marked by the same curiosity that borders on the invasion of privacy and the transgression of personal space. In 'A girl. Scoliotic', she begins with the confession "I don't remember her name./ I remember her Instagram handle. sco.lio/-something. I remember clicking on her/ to compare her/ curves to mine. " In this virtual encounter, the social media profile representing the individual becomes the object of the speaker's scrutiny and realizing that 'my curve/ was never that curvy', she offers a mirror-reaction to socio-cultural perceptions of her own identity.

The cold professionalism of medical procedures and the seeming detachment or unconcern of medical practitioners that work together to objectify the dis-eased body, establish themselves strongly in these poems – "I think a lot about the cold, wet plaster./ And the hands of the doctor/ moulding it around my waist." ('In this one you win') In 'The day of the fitting', the doctor at the Spinal Injuries Hospital who 'does not look at me. He says namaste to Mom' is, paradoxically, also the one whose hands 'messing' with plaster across her torso intimately gather "the skeleton of my body. In his hands/ the silence of my spine, white and hollow. "

In the two poems 'What your doctor will not tell you:' and 'What your doctor will tell you:', Joshi compresses with remarkable skill and deftness the two sides of the experience of embodiment – the private and the public, the subjective and the objective, the circular and the linear, and most importantly, the marginal and the mainstream. The doctor's *"Kuch nahin hota hai"* and *"Lacheeli"* (with regard to the spine), find their alternative truths in the speaker's "Hard-back chairs will hurt no matter what. " and "Do not listen to 'Sexy Back'".

A hint of the Father as Patriarch lurks decisively in this collection in the speaker's equivocal relationship to male figures of reverence and in her repeated seeking for comfort among women. There is the father who, because he is absent in 'Nani's house', the children are "free to dream". In 'The protector of life', Joshi writes:

> …The protector of life
> is a man, and I
> am not surprised. Neither are you.
> I assure you. God

was a man too. This is what we
were given, you and I, Eves weeded out
of the garden of life.

In 'Enter a garden in new delhi', she contrasts the injunctions placed on the female body with the careless freedom of male bodies that manage to remain beyond cultural surveillance– "all around you there are/men/ spread/men spread out/spread all around/legsflopping backssprawling/handscratching bodiesrelaxing" In 'Five stages', the speaker asks "Is it odd to extend responsibility/ for my body?" and the unarticulated answer is 'no' since our bodies are continually being transformed and redefined both physically and psychologically by our personal and social encounters.

With its articulate language, assertive voice, and sharp images, Kuhu Joshi's *My Body Didn't Come Before Me* makes a potent debut, emphasizing subjective embodiment as a form of resistance, and offering an alternate cultural site to reimagine normativity.

The Multiplicity of Heritage: Malashri Lal's *Mandalas of Time*

The word 'debut' is likely to hold different meanings for different people. In general, a certain sense of tentativeness characterises the word, a certain apprehension about how it articulates one's vision of the world and how this is received. When, however, a debut collection of poems comes from a well-known academic, committed feminist, and seasoned reader of poetry like Malashri Lal, the idea of 'debut' is bound to introduce and generate new connotations.

Malashri Lal's *Mandalas of Time* (Hawakal Publishers, 2023), as its title amply suggests, has long been in the making, and even a cursory glance at the seventy-five poems constituting the book will establish its epistemological soundness and firm philosophical depth. Lal's poems, evidently, come from substantial periods of gestation for even when they take off from isolated thought-incidents, they bespeak a roundedness that is accomplished by their being part of a well-assimilated and articulated value-system.

For readers who have received their early lessons in Indian feminisms from the work of scholars like Kamla

Bhasin, Malashri Lal, Sanjukta Dasgupta, Sukrita Paul Kumar, and Sharmila Rege among others, Lal's debut collection of poems, building itself on her rich critical oeuvre, offers significant food for feminist thought. Embodying a vision of the world that is essentially at odds with patriarchy and with radical versions of feminism, *Mandalas of Time* espouses an ethics of inclusiveness and mindfulness that go beyond conventional notions of equity and justice.

Within the vortex of *Mandalas*, one is aware of stepping into a different frame of vision and experience. The idea of time is central to these poems in more ways than one. There is, of course, the title with its mystical suggestions of whorls of time, and the cyclical nature of historicity that is never far from the book's consciousness. But more significantly, *Mandalas*, by weaving together myth and modernity, offers us insights into ever-present civilisational time and its ebbs and flows which have ceaselessly kept their rhythms across ages. Thus, Manthara is honoured as the mother who is uncompromising in raising her daughter as a queen, Shila Devi of Amber as the essential migrant, Radha as a flute devoid of its player, and Sita, waiting for motherhood, as Earth itself that upholds all forms of life in loving and delicate balance.

To read these poems and not notice their thematic and stylistic tenderness would be a huge miss for any reader. In making a point, Lal is never loud or aggressive and yet, there can be no doubt that her points are effectively made. In 'Escape' for instance, an entire narrative of domestic abuse is deftly arranged in a few telling details - "Unseasonal yet so predictable/ So much of a pattern." The return of the protagonist as she "unlocks the suitcase while shutting her heart", having been "struck dumb by the quiet controlling powers", is a repetitive act of courage that Lal refuses to theorise, letting readers find their own contexts of interpretation.

In most poems in this collection, Lal steadily deflects attention from problems to solutions, from what engenders crises to how they might best be handled, from why they exist to how they can be vanquished. Her feminist praxis does not uphold gender equality as the only social ideal but like several feminist writers before her, she draws attention to qualities that women alone possess and which need to be effectively developed and exercised in life's challenging terrain. Concluding an essay on George Eliot for *The Times Literary Supplement*, 20th November, 1919, Virginia Woolf writes of women's particular inheritance - "the difference of view, the difference of standard". In Lal's poems, one comes across this inheritance again and again as the past and present are assessed and reinterpreted in terms of each other.

Examining the collection from a feminist perspective offers its own distinctive rewards, for in these poems, one comes across a model of feminism that is assimilative, accommodative, and committedly empathetic without the radical needs for assertive victimhood, retributive rage, or blistering subversion. Courage, fortitude, truth-telling, comprehensive vision, and empathetic role-switching are valued qualities possessed by Lal's characters in these poems. *Mandalas* notably, begins with 'Ardhanareesvara', a poem that, in its aesthetic and spiritual symbolism, intrinsically underlines the spirit of the collection and determines the tone with which it should be approached:

Sages, sculptors, storytellers knew the eternal truth

That form belies essence much of the time
Masculinity and femininity are the same word,
Read in reverse
To denote the other.

Given her wide interest and scholarship in Indian mythology, it is easy for Lal to evoke metaphors and place them appropriately between the past and the present to offer glimpses into what is necessary, sustainable and capable of sustaining. A particular kind of ventriloquism seems to be at work in these poems when characters from the past reach out to respond to the nuanced crises of the present. Thus, Tagore's heroine Shyamoli reminds us of still "troubled feminism struggling/ Between *Poshak* and *Purdah*", the natural world devoid of human beings during the Pandemic becomes Sita's Ashok Vatika, the dancer's hands in 'In Gandhi's Shadow' remind us of "the invisible *charkha*/ The warp and weft of/ India's Independence/ That even today drives us together/And also apart" while "ghosts from Imperial times" continue to haunt the work of scholars at Viceregal Lodge in Shimla.

Lal's world is never divested of nature's presence and benevolence, and an active realization of the interdependence of the human self and the natural world is, for her, integral to one's comprehensive understanding and the experience of solace. Solace or comfort in the world of *Mandalas*, does not merely come from nature's beauty but from a recognition of her essential vitality, her assertive bounty, and her invincible will in the face of human apathy. In delineating place in her poems, it is not so much the details of form that concern Lal as the spirit of her geographical locales. Poems about Jaipur, Kolkata,

Salzburg or Shantiniketan appeal for the way they reflect the speaking persona in these poems, a persona who ceaselessly forges connections between incidents, people, moments and places.

One enters *Mandalas* as one enters a time warp where ideals, ideas and ideologies, plucked from their points of origin, are in random drift. These poems reframe the question of the new within the cyclical discourse of time to assert that, in a way, nothing has ever been new and that all crises have had echoes and mirrors in the past. There is a multiplicity that lies at the heart of the book, an acknowledgement of the infinite selves that inhere within the one, and the multiple legacies of thought and responsibility that work together in the shaping of every individual.

Mandalas is an attempt to acknowledge this complex heritage as to pass it on to readers who are likely to find in it a reflection of their own dilemmas and their own equations of living through them. Inviting us to explore linkages with multimodal yesterdays through myths where the conscious and unconscious selves meet in spiritual vigour, this collection becomes both a testament of the past and a gospel of the future, a record of both the diminishment of the self by the world and the growth of the self through such diminishments.

Songs of Redemption: Mitali Chakravarty's *Flight of the Angsana Oriole*

"Angsanas are flowers that bloom on tall trees. They are a common site in Singapore, where I stay. Golden orioles are almost the same yellow as angsanas. The orioles flying out of the angsanas are a magical sight – almost like a flower that takes flight," writes Mitali Chakravarty introducing her debut collection of poems.

A yellow bird emerging out of a yellow flower to take flight in the endless sky is an image as spectacular as it is precarious, as extraordinary as it is commonplace, and as material as it is mystical. There is a profundity in its suggestions of liberty and possibility, and in its rich shade of yellow is an enticing hopefulness and a sprightly sense of spring that speaks volumes for the world and worldview that watermark this book.

For readers who are acquainted with Mitali's work at and for *Borderless Journal* of which she is the Founding Editor, the seventy-two poems in *Flight of the Angsana Oriole* (Hawakal Publishers, 2023), will be seen to emerge from ideas that run close to her soul and inspire almost all her work as editor and writer – humanity, brotherhood, borderlessness, nature and the nourishing art of love:

> Love that grows
> with age, with corona,
> with cancer
> ...
> Love that stays
> ... bonded forever by an invisible thread ('Love')

A dense lyricism suffused with an equally strong sense of angst permeates these poems that are, in many ways, about home. Here are diasporic journeys through dream and memory into a past that will never be recovered:

> No longer will I be a daughter –
>
> Just a plain little daughter ('For My Father')

They are, at the same time, about homemaking and the reconstruction of the self in new lands. In Mitali's case, home, experienced through a wide globe-trotting across cultures and landscapes, often fuses into the essential realization of the oneness of mankind and in the search of "the inner wiring/ of the human soul, the human spirit,/ that forever soars beyond hate, beyond/ personal space, beyond land divided/ by boundaries, into an eternity of freedom, where the infinite sky stretches...." ('Arbitrary')

Evoking images of Lalon and Tagore, Mitali finds in the universal brotherhood of Man both belonging and healing -- "the sky that unites/ like an awning". ('Independence Days') In poem after poem, she challenges the divisive values of a society that aligns itself under countless banners only to distinguish and separate -- "the ruthless/ rodents masked with human/ faces screaming 'Divide'" ('Death of Lalon')

The empathetic memory of global atrocities against humanity insistently haunts the subconscious of these poems as they strive to delineate everyday emotions of safety, love, hunger, longing, and companionship in the context of such catastrophes, humanizing suffering by converting it from statistical to emotive data. Whether it is war, genocide or partition, the stark narrative contrast between the personal and the political steadily draws Mitali's attention. Against the rhetoric of ideologies and diplomats, she repeatedly exhorts us to analyse the human costs of suffering:

> This loss of homes.
> Rohingyas.
> Ukrainians
> Afghans
> Palastine-Israel.
> People are born in camps
> in no man's land. ('Weaponising Words')

Side by side with the theme of violence, there blossoms in these poems the firm insistence on love and peace. Love, in Mitali's poems, assumes a variety of forms. There is the daughter's love for her parents, the mother's love for her children, the nature-lover's attention to every detail in her workaday world, the humanist's love for mankind, and the mystic's love for God. What is remarkable is how these various versions of love co-exist and converse with each other to create a collage of not just the poet's life but of life as a whole that draws sustenance from all its relationships -- "Which/ came first – the Universe/ or man, woman and child/ and our urges to equalise? " ('Should I be a Tree?')

In the family poems, in particular, in this collection, one comes across an aching metaphysics that seeks to make sense of life by placing it in conjunction with death. Death holds profound fascination for Mitali as she examines it as a dissolution of the bonds of life, and a portal to a different world that is removed from life's blatant injustices -- "This is the end of her weary, worn life. " ('A Free Spirit') Death, in these poems, is both severance and liberation, a cause of both lamentation and rejoicing. It is life's ultimate end and more desirable, perhaps, given its mounting miseries – the deeply cherished "silence of the universe? " ('Tyrannosaurus Shen')

Injustices against women bear a special place in Mitali's circle of empathy as she documents, in several poems, socio-cultural practices that continue to victimize women down the ages – foeticide, infanticide, dowry-deaths, rape, domestic abuse In 'Kali Rise', for instance, she resurrects the image of a weeping Kali to seek civilisational retribution for generations of women's suffering -- "When with Kali-like blood curling cries will the woman fight/ Injustices, Murder and Abuse?" Here are also ecological poems that address global climate change and remind us of the ceaseless sufferings of the Earth-woman.

There are several poems in which the poet negotiates the issue of identity including her own. Identity is a narrative we construct for ourselves or that which is constructed by others and we learn to internalize and accept it sans questioning. Mitali repeatedly interrogates identity as a construct trying to dissociate it into its multiple layers of being and belonging. We are mostly multitudes, her poems insist, offering the universalist notion of the self as a manifestation of the world:

... - a dream –
a whiff of a drift,

a thing,
a creation,
a fantasy ('Fantasy')

There is a great deal of sensuousness about Mitali's verse which is charged with romanticism in its appreciation of beauty as well as its exploration of existential angst. Her images are culled widely from the lush world of nature and her language, as it contours colours, shapes, and emotions, waxes lyrical and sensitive. There is a sense of devastation in this collection but also one of renewal; a sense of annihilation but never far from that of beginning anew. For all the pain and suffering that life has to offer, Mitali does not lose hope in the possibility of rejuvenation, and of a better world built collectively by human effort and vision.

The Flight of the Angsana Oriole, thus, articulates pertinent questions about our times, inviting us to cast off our weariness, pessimism, and apathy in order to make way for a world where children can smile and birds can take flight into the open sky. By conjuring a vision of sunshine and gold, and drawing attention to the metaphysics of life, the book offers a redemptive read for all who will choose to engage with it.

The Seductions of Language: Prerna Gill's *Meanwhile*

There are many places that poetry comes from -- desire, death, dream, memory, sharp sensuous apprehension, the wrist-grip of language's freedom and magic, the joys and fractures of the world that we engage in everyday, the necessity to commit to paper (or to posterity) what weighs upon the heart or head, the existential imperative to express, or the naïve hope of making the world a better place.

In general, the act of poetic creation draws its sap simultaneously from several of these sources. Many a time, however, one of these inspirations is bound to tower over all the rest. In the case of Prerna Gill's *Meanwhile* (HarperCollins, 2023), the mysterious seduction of words combined with an urge to dress the world in impenetrable veils of meaning by conscientiously shuffling the charted signifiers and signifieds of language, seem to offer the veritable will-to-poetry.

One is drawn to the studied casualness of the title which, with its quiet, meditated understatement, purports poetry to be a by-the-way affair, a random afterthought. Nothing could be farther from the truth. In the title as well as in the book as a whole, there is a skilled juxtaposition of two contiguous temporal frames -- the physical and the psychic. The physical frame is the one in which the seemingly significant events of life take place. The psychic frame constitutes the 'meanwhile' of poetry.

This 'meanwhile' is not to be treated lightly for it is in these pockets of found time that the actual business of confronting the self for survival takes place. Here is a drawn-out negotiation with history, experience, emotions, pain, and trauma, and a poignant reconciliation with each of them. The psychological explorations of the 'meanwhile' in this collection are all-absorbing and have the potency to completely obstruct, offset and vanquish the eventful flow of physical time -- "it's always hungry in here" ('An Hour Stays'). Nevertheless, this is not allowed to happen and both frames persist together, their density often overlapping.

If one pays sufficient aural attention, there is to be heard a silent ticking within Prerna's poems, a tense balance between the physical or material and the psychic or mental, that threatens at any moment to collapse – "I sink through deep green waters/ To a cement floor buried/ Under boxes, old chairs, a pantheon in a funk" ('Visit'). The fifty-nine poems in *Meanwhile*, then, manifest themselves as an acknowledgement of this essential fragility of time, balance, and life -- a realization that if the mind's playhouse is affected or darkened, the lights in life's theatre will inevitably be extinguished.

In the author's words, the book is "an attempt to understand the less-than-shiny things that I can't quite ignore any longer. The everyday things. The things that let the shadows in." The paradoxical nature of time, emotional spontaneity and polyphony, the weaving/unweaving of the self, its fragile alignment/dealignment with the world, and the conglomeration of being constitute the thematic canvas of these poems. The cover image of a huge butterfly replacing the forehead and eyes of a human (woman's) face looms to significance here. The symbolic suggestion of an alternative (inward or non-human) vision is hard to rule out (for animals occupy an enviable space in many poems of this collection) even as one is brought to mind of the butterfly effect of causation that operates, perhaps, most relentlessly in the headspace.

The acuteness of experience, the intensity of its processing, and its configuration through terse but often abrupt and abstruse images constitute the three essential prismatic walls of *Meanwhile*. Here is a carefully constructed theatre of the mind where lights and sounds radically transform in meaning through connotative and symbolic suggestions. In much of Prerna's poetry is a semantic and narrative inscrutability that seems to operate as conscious poetic strategy. In the noumenon of these poems is both illumination and construction. Language is both torch and subterfuge, revelation and concealment, statement and retraction so that travelling through these poems is to traverse an experiential space that is deliberately half-lit.

> In 'Unmasked', the poet writes:
> Glaucous moon shivering inches of glass
> She cuts her shape, cuts at it in echo
> Grows it asking after her sons and rent
> The possibility of rain and grandchildren
> And if they glimpsed her first body
> In birthmark, headline, running stitch

Here, as in many of her pieces, the real and the surreal walk together, undistinguished. In 'Chedipe', for instance - "Never could tell if she first saw him/ From behind green bottles or tall grass" - the atmosphere often turns disturbing and sometimes, singularly acherontic. In 'Tributary', the witnessing of the phenomenon of death opens a startling avenue of perception;

> Until his splintering close enough to see
> How easily a tributary is made:
> A young man slipping from the course of the day
> His hours held close as cards

In these poems' handling of the self as subject, one finds little narcissism. The mind that is sculpted by particularity of experience, memory and upheaval of feeling is, to be sure, intensely subjective and yet, the distillation of these experiences in poetry makes way for a rich reading. What animates these poems and renders them more than abstract musings of an idiosyncratic mind is their keen and devout understanding of life's complexity, its essential sense of injustice, and its brief but significant redemptions – "days pressed to currants between/ Pages folded for the edge of winter/And winters still" ('Ant, Grasshopper') or "Things of a hard blue sky yearn/ For the only light they do not share" ('Before This Summer') The use of short, clipped, often dramatic sentences; the frequent avoidance of punctuation; a polished, urban vocabulary; and an essential belief in the lability of time chisel these poems into pieces reflective of a deeper and highly nuanced reality of the mind as of the world.

The collection has several memorable poems. 'Bucketsful', for instance, brilliantly conjures childhood memory, loss, diminishing, and incommunicability through the bulbous image of frogs "Leaping to the rim/ Like it knew a boiling hurry" and ends with words that "balloon my throat and the only ones who would understand them/ Have long skipped town". In 'Trees', the "verdant announcements" of foliage are capable of sustaining life despite its monotony – "Allergies, dry cleaning, soup" so that "in one glance/ The world becomes/ Leaves". 'Autopsy' builds itself around a single cinematic image – "The naked bulb above the table/ Flickered too much" and as a verb, can symbolically extend itself from a person to a situation to life itself. 'The Dollmaker', one of those poems that makes the act of reading this collection inseparable from the recognition of the author's experiences as a woman in the world, skilfully builds up the automated rhythms of a woman's being in a sexist universe.

Meanwhile, thus, offers a whole new world for our absorption, intriguing in its opacity, and plumbing a depth that is accessible only to those who are prepared to lose themselves in the sharp silhouettes of its images. Here is the gradual but steady eclipsing of material geography to throw light upon the imperialism of the psyche and in this, there is a fine and fluid celluloid effect at work. On the wide screen of language, Prerna's images travel with a terse celluloid confidence – aware, both, of being and non-being, of leading the reader through a range of signification that can never be pinned down to conclusion, of living a lie and yet upholding the truth.

As a debut collection of poems, *Meanwhile* stands out for its innovative experimentation with language which borders, often, on the existential, as if sanity and survival depended upon these elaborate linguistic disguises -- the trickery of words, the enticement as well as the connotative distance of images, and the impossibility of locating a referential kernel to crack. In the measured pace of Prerna's poems is a chromatic adventure that navigates the complex terrain of human emotions via a symbolism of shape, feeling and colour illuminating the little-known multiverse of the subconscious – "Square fingers running a pen/ Over prescription or continent" ('Maps') or "You, with nights under your fingernails/ Tell no one how it happened" ('Black').

In the excavated or found space of 'meanwhile' flows a continuous and consistent dialogue between the various selves – the past and the present, the mentor and the mentee, the seeing and the knowing, the forgetful and the cautious, and so on and so forth. When this space transforms itself into the intersubjective bond of poetry it becomes therapeutic, healing both the speaker and the listener from a pain that is deeply shared as inhabitants of a difficult world -- "Some mornings I think of a rabbit with orchid ears/ The stray toms left her in a pit in my stomach/ Filled with lettuce and sweet straw ('Keeping') or "In this way, we are brittle femur/ And like this, we are sky" ('White').

The world will, perhaps, continue to be what it is. Meanwhile, here is a book that promises to be a friend.

Poetry as Pilgrimage: Robin Ngangom's *My Invented Land*

Into the myriad-doored faith of poetry, there are manifold ways to arrive. Some come to it for respite, some for resuscitation, some for refuge. To a lot of us, poetry is therapeutic; to many others, an arsenal; to yet others, an immortal witness. Through what door one seeks admission into poetry's realm is important for the way poetry will speak to us and the kind of poetry we will, in turn, create.

To Robin Ngangom, poetry manifests itself as both companion and quest, currency in circulation and archive, vision and the language to envision it in. "Poetry cannot help anyone to get on in life," he writes, "or make a successful human being out of anyone. But poetry should move us; it should change us in such a manner that we remain no longer the same after we've read a meaningful poem." ('Introduction') As necessary, as native, and as effortless to him as breath, Ngangom's poetry bespeaks an honest and wholehearted engagement with life that is rare.

My Invented Land: New and Selected Poems (Speaking Tiger Books, 2023) is Ngangom's fourth poetry collection. Containing an admirable selection of his work from his three earlier collections *Words and the Silence* (1988), *Time's*

Crossroads (1994) and *The Desire of Roots* (2006) along with more than thirty new poems, this volume brings to us a fascinating diachronic document of Ngangom's steady journey in and with poetry over the last thirty-five years. For readers familiar with his work, this volume is an asset. For those who wish to make an acquaintance with it, the book will be indispensable and an immensely appealing starting point.

In reading Ngangom's poems, one is pleasantly startled, each time, by his distilled sensibility, his linguistic finesse and his inimitable lyrical fecundity. Simplicity is the catchword of these poems. One would be hard put to identify any posturing in Ngangom's poetry. There are no mirages here, no postmodernist obsession with camouflage, no cautious construction of the self or deliberated distance between poet-observer-speaker. Personality, in fact, is such an important accompaniment of these poems that it casts each poem in the resolutely warm light of its familiarity, meeting in poem after poem, an expectation unarticulated but answered.

Self, land and poetry constitute an essential thematic triangle in *My Invented Land* – each theme inevitably leading to the other. For Ngangom, there is no poetry apart from the existential rootedness of the self in (home)land, this relationship being both a prism and a prison through which his sensibility is reflected upon the world – "But where can one run from the homeland,/ where can I flee from your love?" ('The Strange Affair of Robin S. Ngangom') In the best of times, this bond with the land becomes one of gratitude; in spans of torment, a burden he cannot do without; and during moments of reflection, an agonizing search as in 'Poem for Joseph':

> It is never too late to come home.
> But I must first find a homeland
> where I can find myself,
> just a map or even a tree or a stone
> to mark a spot I could return to
> like an animal lifting his leg
> even when there's nothing to return for.

Even love and its exploration through adolescence into manhood which is an important concern in Ngangom's poetry, finds its expression in the distinct foreground and background of the landscape, so much so that be(love)d and land become one:

> Maternal earth,
> generous and callous.
> You untouchable then,
> and invulnerable now;
> all your instincts
> rearranged with
> your scattered hair.
> Were I to trace
> my name on your frosted mirror
>
>   you would quickly efface it with your breath. ('Age and Memory')

There is no denying the sharp political edge of this poetry, its inveterate honesty and its essential inability to water down the truth with fancy or idealism. In 'To Pacha', a moving elegy to Pacha Meetei, one of Manipur's finest writers, Ngangom writes:

> There are no more tears to shed
> in this withered country where they
> kill pregnant women and children; its

nipples have long gone dry, and leering
death walks your homeland.

In 'The Strange Affair of Robin S. Ngangom', patriotism is "admiring the youth who fondles grenades,/ patriotism is proclaiming all men as brothers/ and secretly depriving my brother,/ patriotism is playing the music of guns/ to the child in the womb." 'My Invented Land' writes home as "a gun/ pressed against both temples/ a knock on a night that has not ended/ a torch lit long after the theft/ a sonnet about body counts/ undoubtedly raped/ definitely abandoned/ in a tryst with destiny." The uneasiness between homeland and nation is a palpable presence in the telling use of the phrase 'tryst with destiny' as it is in many of the poems in this book. The golden jubilee of the nation's independence becomes, in '15 August 2008, Northeast India', "fifty years of discrimination festering in the periphery/ with another anniversary of murder and disappearances." In 'My Invented Land', the homeland "has no boundaries./ At cockcrow one day it found itself/ inside a country to its west,/ (on rainy days it dreams looking east/ when its seditionists fight to liberate it from truth.)"

But this is not a poetry of writing back , of witness, of resistance or of conscious activism. *My Invented Land* is a poetry of observation, of quiet but ceaseless self-exploration and self-assessment (the land being an inalienable unit of the self and vice-versa), of lament and of agonized truth-seeking with "only one pair of shoes/ but many roads" ('Saint Edmund's College') One marvels at the beauty of the title, an apposite image for a body of poems that is invested so completely in poetry as this essentially nourishing collection of eighty-two poems is. This invented land, one realizes, is as much Imphal or Manipur or Shillong or the

Northeast of India as it is the land of memory, imagination, hope, language and poetry.

One must take special note of Ngangom's deftness with language in this collection, his mastery over its opulence and crisis, its headiness and its insomnia, its velocity and meditativeness. Much of his poetry is pointedly and joyously literal with little need of metaphor to expand or accentuate his ideas. However, his language arrives from such depth in the soul that lyricism and beauty are innate to it, deluging the reader with an unsurmised assertion of its grandeur in a poem like 'Laitlum' for instance:

> I want to be converted amongst houses kneeling
> in the thick of firs of former lives,
> randomly built without electricity.

It is characteristic of Ngangom to lift what would be, in most hands, a random assortment of prosaic moments and to elevate it, with his heightened attention, into iridescent poetry. Observe the following lines from 'Street Life':

> I've had decadence forced on me.
> I let the rain waste my day, and arriving
> at streets that do not even know my name
> I take off just like that, waving to silhouettes,
> buying drinks for anyone, even primates
> for whom I have no great regard, hating the houses
> which warn of dogs instead of welcoming me.

The new poems in this collection, while retaining a spiritual connect with the poet's earlier work, branches off into greater profundity. Marked by the loneliness, uncertainty and despair of the Pandemic, the language has grown quieter and more serene so that a metaphysical restlessness animates these poems, quiet unlike the earlier ones – "All voyages will be inward from now," ('September') The language of realism mutates here into unexpected symbols and uneasy images that haunt. 'Postcard' written for Jayanta Mahapatra finds "ghosts leaving friends on the road"; in 'Home', a river swirled with "brown waters/ until it died, strangled by garbage"; in 'Flight', "The most vulnerable will sell bodies./ Because in spite of the landmines/ they still shared limbs."

But despite Ngangom's disquiet with the world and his unceasing inquest into its maladies, love remains his avowed and timeless panacea. It is in and through love that human life acquires redemption and as one moves through the collection, one perceives it watermarked by love of many kinds – amorous, passionate, seductive, lustful, nostalgic, mythic, idyllic, ecological, fraternal and forgiving. Every despondency, for the poet, springs from an absence of love and can find an effective resolution in love – love for the beloved, for the homeland, for one's brethren, for humanity, for poetry, and above all, for love itself. "… someone who cannot love is always alone," he writes in his 'Introduction'. In 'Day', he prays for the Pandemic's end so that "a primeval need/ may be restored to us:/ the ability to hold another/ before the day ends." The all-embracive and sustaining religion of love that leads him to fashion each word "from a private hurt"' ('Introduction') can alone right the balance. In 'January', for instance, he believes that "If anyone were so much as to mention a word like 'love'/ everything will fall quietly again as snow."

Poetry, according to Ngangom, "should not merely amuse us or make us think: it should comfort us, and it must heal the heart of man." ('Introduction') With a brilliant introductory essay by the poet (that makes one desperately wish there were more such essays by Indian English poets on their vision and craft) and its timeless verses, *My Invented Land* accomplishes this and more with poise, grace and an unquestionable claim to the glory of its writer in the canon of Indian English poetry, his committed pilgrimage in verse promising to be an inspiration for many poets to come.

The Palliative of Poetry: Sanket Mhatre's *A City Full of Sirens*

> I wait
> weighing words against memories
> memories against poetry
> poetry against noise
> noise against feeling
> feeling against time
> only to arrive
> to the deepest homecoming of words
> - 'Homecoming'

Something irreplaceably urgent yet inconsolably fragile commands the readers' attention in Sanket Mhatre's *A City Full of Sirens* (Hawakal Publishers, 2023),. There is, to begin with, the orderly chaos of the book cover that with its startling depiction of noise and alarm, summons us to a danger that is as neurological as it is existential, as concretely physical as it is metaphysical, and as identifiable as it is, ultimately, anonymous.

> Darkness asphyxiates
> shifting the axis of your soul
> madness froths
> bubbles of hurt
> shadows of shards

inserting lost files of remembrance
pulse rising –
raising a question at boiling point

Here is an understanding of the city as both protagonist and witness, as conquistador and vanquished, as healer and diseased. Mhatre is mostly talking about Mumbai ("Andheri East doesn't realize/ that it is sleeping in a belly of void/ It is only a matter of time/ until all the lights go out") but his city could be "the broken arteries of Kolkata" ('Mid-flight') or precisely any cityscape where life routinely unravels amidst disillusionment, betrayal, threat and hope, every poem to it being "a wound or a flower or a piece of sunshine" "written on the threshold of vulnerability and despair" as "a letter trying to find its own footprint on the shifting axis of time and circumstance" ('Introduction')

Tortuous and tortured, Mhatre's city is a site of bereavement, uncertainty, imperilment, disease, derangement and more, its inhabitants choiceless in their compulsion to wear its frayed fabric upon their skin. But this is not all. Lurking within these poems is also the decisive realization of the city as a human construct, a mirror that reflects rather than distorts or imposes human irresponsibility and disorder. In the title poem of the collection, for instance, the city is a patient incapable of being saved by its nonchalant dwellers:

the city has been suddenly diagnosed with Stage 3C
and all of us who matter to her:
slum dwellers, middle class, uber rich
upper caste, sub-middle-sub-lower, lower,
converts, casteless, outcasts, pimps and city planners
were late by a minimum of ten months in pre-
empting this disease

Mhatre's cities emit steady sirens of disaster – biological, ecological, technological, moral and aesthetic. But redemption, too, is to be found here alone ("Clay hands in a relentless prayer to -/ everything the earth stands for/ and everything that rises upwards from it." - 'A Kiss of Cotton') for only what hurts has the ability to effectively transform – "anything that doesn't change our body can never change us". ('Culture of Transience') What, chiefly, reconciles the city as wound to the city as mirror, is the imperative of language and its expressive potential for love and poetry. ("A verse could be an open road" - 'These Years with Her')

A City Full of Sirens is a dense interrogation of the city, its sirens of overpopulation, congestion, capitalism and climate change, and an exploration of the fullness or plenitude of language that can somehow soften all of this and make it more bearable for life and time. Firmly rooting this collection is a momentous faith in the capacity of words to resist postmodern fragmentation by building bridges across emotions, cultures, and epistemologies. Mhatre's imagination in poetry is luxuriantly metaphorical. In almost every poem, words defy ordinary appearances to transform into winged images in deep conversation with a reality tangential to the page. In 'Anuvaad', as the poet says, all languages are born "from the same birdsong". In 'The Concept of Distance', every stanza offers a new perspective into distance – "The space of pain between two alphabets, now divorced,/ looking on either side of a sentence". In 'Morphing into Everything', the beloved and the city coalesce into one:

> my fortresses crumble
> dissolve mid-sea

rebirth as an archipelago
sink into her navel
populate her mind
germinate on her dermis
disintegrate into a thousand birds
taking early flight

In each of the fifty-six poems in the collection is a seamless interweaving of self and space. Most of Mhatre's sirens are symbolic, conjured through the weight and immediacy of metaphor. In each poem is this sense of something that must be overcome -- a lurking claustrophobia, an unnamed distrust, a haunting faithlessness, a constant suggestion of order tipping into anarchy.

An acute precariousness, marked by a vital need to thresh out feeling on the floor of language,
is the signature of this collection.

Very significantly, many of these poems are about poetry itself -- its genesis, composition, structure, and its relentless shapeshifting ability to weld disparate worlds and subjectivities into a coherent experiential whole. Unravelling within this book's narrative arc is an empathetic journey of the body and spirit, its goal being to discover "the completeness of existence...Time. Tide. Man. Woman. Humanity. Age. Difference. Distance". ('Rain Being') Passion configures these poems in various ways and not least through the erotic of language. In the best poems here, love, poetry, woman and city become indistinguishable from one another, permeating ontological and aesthetic boundaries and accomplishing a spiritual surrealism that marks the distinctness of this collection.

A City Full of Sirens is, thus, about cities that are both germane and antithetical to poetry, about a "confabulated planet" and mutating geographies "stretching/ through thick mesh of bones and arteries/ pulp synchronized to our heartbeats/ birdsong to a breath/ while ink sprawls/ on a dream of half-slept pages". ('Vertical Forests') It is equally about the inhabitants of the cityscape, the reconciliation of their numerous fragments and roles – "a new you added everyday/ an old you subtracted". ('The Queue'), intending "to geolocate/ the fulcrum of our absolute feeling/ outliving erasures". ('Synthesis')

The collection remains remarkable for its obsession with language, its authentic emotional inflections, its charged candour, and its oscillations across a wide thematic range of existence, estrangement, erosion, and redemption. Annihilation, disease and death watermark these poems in undeniable ways but the energy of the book lies in its refusal to be contained within scripts of hopelessness or pain. Summoning optimism to thought and agency to action, *A City Full of Sirens* makes a palliative of poetry and crafts an entourage of life's resilience to learn from every setback –

> I was never the rain.
> Until you cloud-burst me with words.
> You gave me the first drop.
> It's my turn to take you in.
> ('Rain Being')

Black Eagle Books

www.blackeaglebooks.org
info@blackeaglebooks.org

Black Eagle Books, an independent publisher, was founded as a nonprofit organization in April, 2019. It is our mission to connect and engage the Indian diaspora and the world at large with the best of works of world literature published on a collaborative platform, with special emphasis on foregrounding Contemporary Classics and New Writing.

www.ingramcontent.com/pod-product-compliance
Lightning Source LLC
Chambersburg PA
CBHW060559080526
44585CB00013B/627